YO-BRV-012

DISCARD

R - Local History
016.929 Sper
Sperry
Survey of American genealogical
periodicals and periodical indexes

		DATE DUE	

A Survey of American Genealogical Periodicals and Periodical Indexes

GALE GENEALOGY AND LOCAL HISTORY SERIES

Series Editor: J. Carlyle Parker, Head of Public Services and Assistant Library Director, California State College, Stanislaus; and Founder and Librarian Volunteer, Modesto California Branch Genealogical Library of the Genealogical Department of the Church of Jesus Christ of Latter-day Saints, Salt Lake City, Utah

Also in this series:

AMERICAN INDIAN GENEALOGICAL RESEARCH—*Edited by Jimmy B. Parker and Noel R. Barton**

AN INDEX TO THE BIOGRAPHIES IN 19TH CENTURY CALIFORNIA COUNTY HISTORIES—*Edited by J. Carlyle Parker**

BLACK GENESIS—*Edited by James Rose and Alice Eichholz*

BLACKS IN THE FEDERAL CENSUS—*Edited by James Rose and Alice Eichholz**

CITY, COUNTY, TOWN, AND TOWNSHIP INDEX TO THE 1850 FEDERAL CENSUS SCHEDULES—*Edited by J. Carlyle Parker**

COMPENDIUMS OF QUAKER GENEALOGICAL RESEARCH—*Edited by Willard Heiss**

GENEALOGICAL HISTORICAL GUIDE TO LATIN AMERICA—*Edited by Lyman De Platt*

GENEALOGICAL RECORDS OF BLACKS IN SOUTHEASTERN CONNECTICUT, 1650-1900—*Edited by James Rose and Barbara Brown**

GENEALOGICAL RESEARCH FOR CZECH AND SLOVAK AMERICANS—*Edited by Olga K. Miller*

LIBRARY SERVICE FOR GENEALOGISTS—*Edited by J. Carlyle Parker**

MENNONITE GENEALOGICAL RESEARCH—*Edited by Delbert Gratz**

MONTANA'S GENEALOGICAL RECORDS—*Edited by Dennis L. Richards**

A PERSONAL NAME INDEX TO ORTON'S "RECORDS OF CALIFORNIA MEN IN THE WAR OF THE REBELLION, 1861 TO 1867"—*Edited by J. Carlyle Parker*

WESTERN CANADIAN GENEALOGICAL RESEARCH—*Edited by Jimmy B. Parker and Noel R. Barton**

*in preparation

General Editor: Paul Wasserman, Professor and former Dean, School of Library and Information Services, University of Maryland

Managing Editor: Denise Allard Adzigian, Gale Research Company

A Survey of American Genealogical Periodicals and Periodical Indexes

Volume 3 in the Gale Genealogy and Local History Series

Kip Sperry

*Technical Writer and
United States Research Specialist
Genealogical Society
Salt Lake City, Utah*

Gale Research Company
Book Tower, Detroit, Michigan 48226

Library of Congress Cataloging in Publication Data

Sperry, Kip.
  A survey of American genealogical periodicals and periodical indexes.

  (Gale genealogy and local history series; v. 3)
  Bibliography: p. 184
  Includes indexes.
    1. United States--Genealogy--Periodicals--Indexes--Bibliography. 2. United
States--Genealogy--Periodicals--Bibliography. I. Title.
Z5313.U5S65   [CS42]   016.929'1'05   78-55033
ISBN 0-8103-1401-0

VITA

Kip Sperry is employed as a technical writer and United States research specialist at the Genealogical Society in Salt Lake City, Utah. He is an Accredited
Genealogist and specialist in the following regions: New England states, East-
ern (Middle-Atlantic) states, and Midwestern states.

A member of the Board of Directors of the Utah Genealogical Association, he
is editor of their publication, the GENEALOGICAL JOURNAL, and has been
a contributing editor and an associate editor to this periodical. He has author-
ed many articles and also book reviews for various genealogical periodicals.
He has lectured at various genealogical seminars and teaches classes in American genealogical research at the Brigham Young University Salt Lake Center.
Sperry is a member of several genealogical societies and has attended a number
of genealogical seminars, including one at the National Archives. He has performed original research throughout the United States in many libraries and
genealogical repositories.

He has compiled INDEX TO THE GENEALOGICAL JOURNAL, VOLUMES 1-5,
1972-1976; A GUIDE TO INDEXES TO MORMON WORKS, MORMON COL-
LECTIONS, AND UTAH COLLECTIONS; and a seventeen-year composite index
to American genealogical periodical literature. His Master's thesis is related
to the subject of this work and is entitled A STUDY OF BIBLIOGRAPHICAL
CONTROL OF UNITED STATES GENEALOGICAL PERIODICAL LITERATURE.

Sperry received a Master's degree in Library and Information Sciences from
Brigham Young University in Provo, Utah. He also has A.S. and B.S. degrees
in genealogy from BYU, where he specialized in American research

CONTENTS

LIST OF ILLUSTRATIONS

List of Illustrations

PREFACE

A number of American genealogical periodicals and historical periodicals with genealogical data have been published since the middle of the nineteenth century. An overwhelming volume of genealogical material is contained in these publications. Information in these periodicals includes solutions to countless genealogical research problems.

How does one gain access to the contents of current and retrospective genealogical periodicals? What are the uses and limitations of genealogical periodical literature? How does one effectively use indexes to periodicals? This work seeks to answer these questions.

A systematic research approach is described whereby the genealogist includes periodical literature and composite indexes to the literature as part of his research technique. The importance of genealogical periodicals as a source is examined. Also discussed is their use and relationship to the beginning stages of genealogical research. The major indexes to American genealogical periodicals are then described. Bibliographies and reference sources are shown throughout the book. Appendixes containing titles of valuable genealogical indexes and bibliographies are included. An extensive listing of titles of American genealogical periodicals is contained in appendix 3.

Written primarily for American genealogists, as well as librarians with a genealogical collection, the work should also prove useful to historians and others concerned with American genealogy and local history. Some sources of interest to British genealogists are mentioned. This survey should serve as a helpful reference tool.

Appreciation is expressed to my wife, Elisabeth Anne Pearson Sperry, who has been of invaluable assistance in reading the manuscript and in offering helpful criticism. Special thanks are also due to George Ely Russell, of Middletown, Maryland, and Roger Scanland, of Salt Lake City, for their assistance in reading the manuscript.

Kip Sperry

FOREWORD

We did not invent genealogy. Late comers all, we are but the most recent workers in a field of knowledge which has been under study for centuries. While we may boast of our enlightened modern methodology, the foundations of most of our work, standards, and practices were laid by our predecessors.

There are among us some genealogical purists who look with disdain at our periodical literature, insisting that true genealogy must derive only from research in original documentary records. They would have us believe that, prior to their appearance on the scene, no writer of journal articles had sufficient skill or access to information to arrive at sound conclusions.

But we do not have to reinvent the wheel. Almost every conceivable genealogical subject, be it an immigrant family or a research technique, has been dealt with by our predecessors. The results of their work are now a part of our body of literature. This printed information is now so immense and dispersed that much of it is inaccessible, forgotten, lost, or ignored. There is no single central depository for all genealogical books and periodicals, no catalog, no index.

How then may we retrieve and exploit prior work and findings? This is a problem which is addressed in part by this survey. Mr. Sperry, a professional genealogical reference librarian as well as a genealogist and records searcher, with years of experience (and frustration) in attempting to unlock our literature, has come to grips with the problem. In the following pages he points out the wisdom of making a preliminary search of the periodical literature, describes that literature, analyzes the available indexes, provides guidance for most effective use of the indexes, and suggests needed improvements in information retrieval tools. Other useful information is appended to this work, which is commended to your attention.

GEORGE ELY RUSSELL, Certified Genealogist;
Editor, NATIONAL GENEALOGICAL SOCIETY
QUARTERLY, and GENEALOGICAL PERIODICAL
ANNUAL INDEX, 1966-69
Middletown, Maryland

Chapter 1

THE SURVEY: AN INTRODUCTION
TO GENEALOGICAL RESEARCH

America's Bicentennial and Alex Haley's ROOTS have kindled increasing aware-
ness and appreciation for family and local history. We are seeing a large
number of family genealogies, historical accounts, biographies, and other tradi-
tional aspects of historical and genealogical research. The varying quality of
these publications points out the need for a fundamental understanding of the
complexities of genealogical research. This book attempts to define one specialized aspect of genealogical research.

When approached logically, genealogical research can be a fascinating pursuit.
However, success depends largely upon the genealogist's familiarity with basic
research sources and procedures. This chapter focuses on a systematic method
of beginning genealogical research.

THE SURVEY

Basically, genealogical research consists of two phases of activity: (1) the survey phase, which involves searching home sources, published materials, and
other compiled or secondary sources, and (2) the research phase, which usually
consists of searching primary sources and some additional secondary materials.
A primary source is defined as one created by someone directly involved with
the event and recorded at or near the time of that event. An example is a
church register containing genealogical information recorded close to the time
of the event, such as a christening, marriage, or burial. Secondary sources,
on the other hand, are recorded some time after the event or they are in printed format. Examples of secondary sources include compiled genealogies, family
histories, local histories, genealogical periodicals, and indexes to works, including indexes to genealogical periodicals as well as indexes to other sources.

Before commencing intensive genealogical research into original records such
as parish registers; court, census, and land records; tax lists; and military or
immigration records, the genealogist might do well to determine first whether
or not research has been performed by others on the selected pedigree problem.
One approach is to perform a "preliminary survey."

1

Introduction to Genealogical Research

The function of a preliminary survey--sometimes termed a research survey or pedigree survey--is to determine, synthesize, and analyze the value and extent of previous research on a pedigree line.

The genealogist does not attempt to establish facts beyond a reasonable doubt during the survey; rather, data are gathered from survey sources in order to determine what has already been accomplished on the pedigree objective. Verification of the information located during the survey is advisable. This can be done by searching original records and well-documented secondary sources.

As the genealogist performs a survey and begins research in original records, he becomes acquainted with various types of sources. He should be aware of the following key elements: time period, content, availability, genealogical applications, and limitations. It is important for the researcher to analyze carefully the uses and limitations of each genealogical source being used to solve research problems.

Information revealed by a preliminary survey will not always be accurate. Nevertheless, data found in a survey will often guide the genealogist to records containing more dependable information. A genealogical survey helps establish proper research dimensions and parameters.

In genealogical research, one should work from the known to the unknown as is done in other research disciplines. The genealogical research method includes three general steps: (1) selecting a survey or research objective (goal), (2) searching pertinent survey and original records which might solve the stated objective, and (3) evaluating and analyzing the evidence obtained from the sources searched. It is realized, however, that this process is more complex, particularly when performing original research. Other steps in the research process in addition to those listed might include determining appropriate sources to search, locating the sources, and recording and using the results.

These steps can be used in both the survey phase and the research phase and should be followed in all genealogical research problems. Each time evidence is evaluated and analyzed, a new objective is selected, additional records are searched, and another evaluation is made.

When a previously unknown personal name is discovered in survey or research sources, the researcher should begin the survey phase anew for that particular name. As new data are located, it will be necessary for the researcher to recheck survey sources for information which was previously unknown.

Sources which should be carefully and systematically searched during the preliminary survey include those contained in the following three categories: (1) family and home sources, (2) special indexes and collections available in genealogical repositories, and (3) printed sources, such as family and local histories, biographies, genealogical periodical literature, and related indexes to the literature. Most of these sources are secondary in nature.

2

Family and Home Sources

Those who are just launching a search of their ancestry should begin by obtaining facts about the immediate family. This information should be placed in a notebook, or on a family group record, a pedigree chart, or a similar form. Relatives should be interviewed as part of the survey, particularly elderly family members. They should be contacted in person or by correspondence in order to learn as much information as possible about the family. It will be helpful to tape-record conversations with older members of the family.

Correspondence should be initiated with pertinent national, state, and local officials, genealogical and historical societies, and others who may be of assistance in extending the pedigree. Copies of vital records (births, marriages, and deaths) should be obtained, when available. Collections in libraries and record repositories are part of the survey, and these should also be systematically investigated.

When available, a search of the following types of home sources, either in person or by correspondence, should be undertaken as an initial step in the survey:

    family Bibles
    family histories (including genealogies and biographies)
    letters (particularly older letters which contain genealogical information)
    certificates of vital statistical information
    journals, scrapbooks, and diaries
    photographs
    newspaper clippings (especially obituaries)
    school records
    military and pension records
    land and property records
    wills and probate records
    citizenship and naturalization records
    memorial and funeral cards

As the pedigree is extended, family and home sources become less significant as a source. The value of searching home sources depends upon the time period of the ancestral problem.

Family traditions are often useful in beginning research. However, those traditions should be used with some caution, since they usually become distorted through the years. Nevertheless, family traditions may offer important clues to further searching. For example, the family may have handed down the belief that a particular ancestor belonged to the Quaker religion, or some other religious affiliation. This may or may not be true. One tradition which can sometimes be proven incorrect is that the immigrant ancestor "came from England with two brothers."

Indexes and Special Collections in Libraries

Indexes and special genealogical collections can be found in various genealogical and historical repositories. Many libraries have genealogical collections
containing an assortment of helpful survey sources. After home records have
been thoroughly searched, the researcher should seek such library collections.
Collections of interest to genealogists are found in many public libraries, historical and genealogical society libraries, special and university libraries, church
and state archives, and similar repositories. One should also be aware of the
extensive genealogical sources at the Library of Congress and the National Archives in Washington, D.C.

Libraries which house these valuable collections may be located in the research-
er's area of residence, in the area of the research problem, or in major cities.
Many of these are well-known genealogical libraries such as the New York City
Public Library; the New England Historic and Genealogical Society, Boston;
the Newberry Library, Chicago; or the Genealogical Society Library, Salt Lake
City.[1]

Survey sources available in some of the above-mentioned libraries include indexes to genealogical, historical, or other collections; printed sources, including family histories; family group records; pedigree charts; and various other
specialized genealogical collections, including manuscript collections. The indexes in these libraries can be used in conjunction with printed materials or
original sources in that particular library, or they may refer the researcher to
collections in another repository. Through bibliographic tools the librarian will
then be able to put the patron in contact with the repository which has the appropriate source to which the index refers.

In addition to the card catalog, libraries and genealogical and historical society
libraries have special card or other indexes which are helpful to researchers;
many indexes are peculiar to that library. Special indexes to genealogical collections should be checked as part of the preliminary survey. Sources which
may be listed in such special indexes include printed materials, such as family
and local histories, genealogical periodicals and newspapers; and original records, such as family Bibles, and church, census, land, and court records.
Other valuable genealogical sources may also be indexed and available in local libraries. It is the genealogist's task to seek out and make use of these
materials.

Indexes guide the researcher into primary and secondary sources, depending upon the type and content of the index. Many times secondary sources, especially those which are well documented, will direct the researcher to primary
sources. The ultimate objective in locating genealogical sources is to locate
appropriate primary sources when available. Indexes and secondary sources can
help reach this objective.

4

Printed Sources

There are numerous printed sources available to genealogists, and these should be systematically searched during the survey phase. This is often known as a literature search. Searching printed sources is an important part of the survey. It may be possible to locate biographical and genealogical information concerning one's ancestry in sources such as family histories and genealogies, both in printed and manuscript form; local histories, especially county histories and biographies; genealogical periodical literature; and similar biographical materials. A number of these secondary sources have been at least partially indexed. Some are extremely well indexed, usually by personal names but may also be indexed by subjects and locality references.

As might be expected, printed sources must be used cautiously. There is always a chance for printing errors, or errors on the part of the compiler. Some printed genealogies are well documented, while others lack any sort of documentation. The genealogist should determine what sources were used in the compilation.

CONCLUSION

Genealogy is the study of individual or family descent with particular emphasis on personal names, dates, place names, and relationships. These four key elements are essential in identifying ancestors, either in the survey phase or in the research phase. Determining the sex of an individual is also an important consideration. Occupations may also be useful to know.

A survey should be performed before beginning intensive genealogical research into original records. A preliminary survey lays the foundation for more advanced genealogical research. Often both time and expense can be saved by performing a survey.

When a new ancestral name is located during the survey phase or research phase, the genealogist should begin the survey again for that particular name. It is often necessary to recheck survey sources for information which was previously unknown.

Pedigree problems should be defined and solved systematically as they are encountered. The results of the survey should be analyzed before beginning research into original records. During the survey, the researcher should note any conflicting or insufficient evidence on the pedigree. Steps can then be outlined to solve the problem.

Disappointment and frustration can be avoided if the genealogist will acquire a basic knowledge of genealogical research procedures. This includes a general understanding of the entire research cycle, a familiarity with record sources in the area of the research problem, a knowledge of the history of the area of the research problem, an ability to read and interpret the handwriting of the time period of the problem, an ability to properly evaluate the evidence, a basic knowledge of library science, and other factors, which may include a knowledge of a foreign language.

SUPPLEMENTARY READINGS

This section includes a selected bibliography of useful reference sources, periodical articles, and genealogical textbooks which further define the survey and research phases. Some of these sources discuss, with varying viewpoints, the use and importance of primary and secondary sources in genealogical research, and expand the concepts discussed in this chapter. Many will be available at libraries with a genealogical collection.

An introduction to the survey phase and its relationship to the total genealogical research process has been presented in this chapter. Record-keeping systems, the intricacies of evaluating evidence, selection of pedigree objectives, effective use of correspondence, the location of specific records, paleography (the study of old handwriting), and other fundamental aspects of genealogical research activity have not been described. These are adequately covered in several of the following sources. Examples of pedigree charts, family group records (family unit forms), and other aspects of record-keeping systems are shown in some of the sources cited.

These sources will be of particular interest to American genealogists. United States and Canadian local, state, regional, and national genealogical sources, and other specialized topics, are discussed in some of these writings.

Adams, Golden V., Jr. "The Genealogical Research Process." GENEALOGICAL JOURNAL 1-2 (1972-73): 59-65, 95-98; 10-14, 59-61.

American Genealogical Research Institute. HOW TO TRACE YOUR FAMILY TREE. Arlington, Va.: 1973; Garden City, N.Y.: Doubleday, 1975.

American Society of Genealogists. GENEALOGICAL RESEARCH. 2 vols. Vol. 1 edited by Milton Rubincam; vol. 2 edited by Kenn Stryker-Rodda. Washington, D.C.: 1960, 1971.

Bennett, Archibald F. ADVANCED GENEALOGICAL RESEARCH. Salt Lake City: Bookcraft, 1959.

_____. FINDING YOUR FOREFATHERS IN AMERICA. Salt Lake City: Bookcraft, 1957.

_____. A GUIDE FOR GENEALOGICAL RESEARCH. 2d ed. Salt Lake City: Genealogical Society of The Church of Jesus Christ of Latter-day Saints, 1960.

Cox, Evelyn. "Where to Begin, and How, in Genealogy Research." TRI-STATE TRADER, 7 February 1976, pp. 37, 40.

Daughters of the American Revolution. Genealogical Advisory Committee to the Registrar General. IS THAT LINEAGE RIGHT? Washington, D.C.: National Society of the Daughters of the American Revolution, 1965.

Dismukes, Camillus J. "Aids for the Family Historian: Mechanics, Pitfalls, and Concepts of Genealogy." NATIONAL GENEALOGICAL SOCIETY QUARTERLY 57 (1969): 163-78.

Doane, Gilbert H. SEARCHING FOR YOUR ANCESTORS: THE HOW AND WHY OF GENEALOGY. 4th ed. Minneapolis: University of Minnesota Press, 1973; New York: Bantam Books, 1974.

Everton, George B., Sr., ed. THE HANDY BOOK FOR GENEALOGISTS. 6th ed., rev. and enl. Logan, Utah: Everton Publishers, 1971.

_____. THE HOW BOOK FOR GENEALOGISTS. 7th ed. Logan, Utah: Everton Publishers, 1971.

Fudge, George H., and Smith, Frank. LDS GENEALOGIST'S HANDBOOK: MODERN PROCEDURES AND SYSTEMS. Salt Lake City: Bookcraft, 1972.

Greenwood, Val D. THE RESEARCHER'S GUIDE TO AMERICAN GENEALOGY. Baltimore: Genealogical Publishing Co., 1973.

Harland, Derek. GENEALOGICAL RESEARCH STANDARDS. Salt Lake City: Bookcraft, 1963. Formerly A BASIC COURSE IN GENEALOGY, VOL. 2.

Helmbold, F. Wilbur. TRACING YOUR ANCESTRY: A STEP-BY-STEP GUIDE TO RESEARCHING YOUR FAMILY HISTORY. Birmingham, Ala.: Oxmoor House, 1976.

Jacobus, Donald Lines. GENEALOGY AS PASTIME AND PROFESSION. 2d rev. ed. Baltimore: Genealogical Publishing Co., 1968.

_____. "To Trace Your Ancestry." THE AMERICAN GENEALOGIST 40 (1964): 240-45.

Jaussi, Laureen R., and Chaston, Gloria D. FUNDAMENTALS OF GENEALOGICAL RESEARCH. 3d rev. ed. Salt Lake City: Deseret Book Co., 1977.

Jones, Vincent L.; Eakle, Arlene H.; and Christensen, Mildred H. GENEALOGICAL RESEARCH: A JURISDICTIONAL APPROACH. Rev. ed. in paperback. Salt Lake City: Publishers Press, 1972. Reissued as FAMILY HISTORY FOR FUN AND PROFIT.

Kirkham, E. Kay. PROFESSIONAL TECHNIQUES AND TACTICS IN AMERI-CAN GENEALOGICAL RESEARCH. Logan, Utah: Everton Publishers, 1973.

_____. RESEARCH IN AMERICAN GENEALOGY. Salt Lake City: Deseret Book Co., 1956.

_____. SIMPLIFIED GENEALOGY FOR AMERICANS. Salt Lake City: Deseret Book Co., 1968.

Miller, Beverly B. "Discovering Genealogy." WESTERN NEW YORK GENEA-LOGICAL SOCIETY JOURNAL 2 (1975): 118-20.

Nichols, Elizabeth L. THE GENESIS OF YOUR GENEALOGY. 2d ed. Logan, Utah: Everton Publishers, 1973.

_____. HELP IS AVAILABLE. Logan, Utah: Everton Publishers, 1972.

St. Louis Genealogical Society. AN'QUEST'ORS: A GUIDE TO TRACING YOUR FAMILY TREE. St. Louis: 1971.

Skalka, Lois Martin. TRACING, CHARTING AND WRITING YOUR FAMILY HISTORY. New York: Pilot Books, 1975.

Sperry, Kip. "First, Survey Your Pedigree Problem before Research Phase Be-gins." TRI-STATE TRADER, 16 November 1974, p. 38.

Stevenson, Noel C. SEARCH AND RESEARCH. Salt Lake City: Deseret Book Co., 1977.

Vallentine, John F. "Pedigree Analysis and Research Planning." GENEA-LOGICAL JOURNAL 3 (1974): 92-95.

White, Elizabeth Pearson. "Constructive Imagination in Family Research." ILLINOIS STATE GENEALOGICAL SOCIETY QUARTERLY 7 (1975): 96-102.

Williams, Ethel W. KNOW YOUR ANCESTORS: A GUIDE TO GENEALOGI-CAL RESEARCH. Rutland, Vt.: Charles W. Tuttle Co., 1971.

Wolf, Joseph C. "The Tools and Technique of Genealogical Research." INDI-ANA MAGAZINE OF HISTORY 38 (1942): 93-105. Reprinted in GENEALOGY BEGINNER'S MANUAL, Ft. Wayne Public Library, 1975.

Wright, Norman Edgar. BUILDING AN AMERICAN PEDIGREE: A STUDY IN GENEALOGY. Provo, Utah: Brigham Young University Press, 1974.

_____, ed. GENEALOGICAL READER: NORTHEASTERN UNITED STATES AND CANADA. Provo, Utah: Brigham Young University Press, 1973.

Wright, Norman E[dgar], and Pratt, David H. GENEALOGICAL RESEARCH ESSENTIALS. Salt Lake City: Bookcraft, 1967.

Zabriskie, George Olin. CLIMBING OUR FAMILY TREE SYSTEMATICALLY. Salt Lake City: Parliament Press, 1969.

NOTES

1. Genealogical Society of The Church of Jesus Christ of Latter-day Saints, 50 East North Temple, Salt Lake City, Utah 84150.

Chapter 2

AMERICAN GENEALOGICAL PERIODICAL LITERATURE

VALUE OF SEARCHING THE LITERATURE

Before beginning an intensive genealogical research program, the researcher should, whenever possible, review the periodical literature concerning the area of the research problem. This procedure should become a systematic part of one's research methodology.

Milton Rubincam, a prominent American genealogist, emphasized the importance of reviewing periodical literature before beginning a research problem:

Many errors would be avoided if the compilers of genealogies would take the trouble to familiarize themselves with genealogical magazines . . . it is a good policy to review the periodical literature devoted to this type of research. . . .

The value of occasionally reviewing the periodical literature is twofold: (1) Articles dealing with family history are thus brought to our attention, and (2) we often find source-materials (tombstone inscriptions, Bible records, church registers, etc.) and guides to research in our ancestral areas which otherwise would escape us entirely.[1]

Noel C. Stevenson selected and edited a collection of genealogical articles and these were published in THE GENEALOGICAL READER. He makes several important statements in the preface to this anthology:

Hidden away in the various genealogical periodicals are many excellent articles on genealogical research, . . . Many of these writings on genealogy are masterpieces that delineate research methods in an extremely lucid style. These articles have fulfilled a need in supplying the necessary background every researcher must acquire before he can become a competent genealogist. . . . A genealogical researcher who has not read and digested material on interpreting records, problems involving the calendar, official records, new developments in research, critical analyses of subjects such as heraldry, pre-American ancestry, and identification of ancestors, is simply not keeping current with his subject.[2]

Genealogical Periodical Literature

Genealogical periodicals are a valuable source of instruction and information for both the advanced and the beginning genealogist. These periodicals often publish articles defining genealogical research principles and procedures similar in scope to those found in genealogical textbooks. Reading genealogical periodicals will assist the genealogist in obtaining a background in genealogy, history, and related disciplines. It is not unusual to find information in these periodicals which is unavailable elsewhere, or which may not be readily available to researchers in any other printed format. Corrections to published genealogies are sometimes published in periodicals.

A knowledge of and familiarity with the current literature is an integral part of a professional genealogist's self-development. Reading genealogical periodicals and newsletters--especially those published in the locality or localities of the genealogist's research specialization--is essential for keeping abreast of the newest developments in the field of genealogy.

Receiving genealogical periodicals and newsletters is one of the benefits of belonging to genealogical and historical societies, since most such organizations publish this type of literature. Newsletters are especially useful since they often contain up-to-date information on newly available genealogical sources, use of record sources, book reviews, and similar items. Genealogical periodical literature and indexes to the literature will be a welcome addition to one's private library. Genealogists should belong to genealogical organizations and subscribe to those genealogical periodicals of importance to their area(s) of research specialization--especially those periodicals not found in libraries in the vicinity of the genealogist's residence.

The usefulness and value of genealogical periodical literature cannot be over-emphasized. Countless genealogical research problems could be solved by searching appropriate genealogical serials. Locating selected family names or locality records in a periodical may lead the researcher to additional genealogical information, including clues to other record sources and references to original records where more data would be available.

The genealogical time period covered in an American genealogical periodical article might be from early colonial days, or earlier, to the present generation, even if the periodical was published in 1875, 1925, or 1975. In other words, a recent publication might very well include genealogical data on one's grandparents, or possibly one's fourth great-grandparents.

The difficulty of locating these data lies in the fact that such information is often buried in a relatively unknown article or publication, making the information very difficult to find. One solution to the problem of accessibility of these hidden data lies in the proper use of indexes to genealogical periodical literature. By making use of the available periodical indexes, it is possible to identify such buried material.

CONTENTS OF GENEALOGICAL PERIODICALS

Neatly entombed in genealogical and historical periodicals published in the United States and Canada are thousands of personal names, dates, published locality records, and other information of interest to genealogists and historians. Although the contents of these periodicals vary from one publication to another, some of the following may be contained in a typical issue of a genealogical periodical:

1. family histories, pedigrees, or compiled genealogies (documented or undocumented)
2. abstracts or extracts from various original record sources, such as family Bibles, court and probate records, guardianships, emigration/ immigration records, naturalizations, tombstone inscriptions or cemetery records, vital records (births, marriages, deaths), church records (christenings, marriages, burials, memberships, etc.), land records, census records, military records, tax lists, letters and other family records, civil records, personal records (such as doctors' records, journals, ledgers, account books, and other business records), indexes to records, and information republished from printed sources such as newspapers (e.g., obituaries)
3. biographical sketches of deceased members or ancestors of deceased members of the organization associated with the periodical
4. instructions on the use of various genealogical or historical sources, whether ethnic, national, regional, or local in scope
5. descriptions of record sources and collections
6. articles concerning research methodology and research experiences
7. articles offering advice on solving genealogical problems, teaching classes, establishing a family organization, or publishing family histories
8. articles concerning little-known genealogical or historical sources, discovery of sources, or lists of available sources
9. articles explaining the historical background of localities
10. articles, news notes, or mention of events or people
11. indexes, especially to records previously unindexed
12. indexes to that particular magazine (i.e., personal name, subject, locality, or query indexes)
13. book reviews (critical book reviews or book notices)
14. announcements of new publications of interest to genealogists
15. genealogical queries (inquiries) and sometimes answers to published queries[3]
16. heraldic information (articles or advertisements concerning coats of arms and other aspects of heraldry)
17. advertisements (such as advertisements by private genealogists, genealogical research companies, publishers of genealogical materials or microfilm rental companies, family organizations, genealogical/historical societies, or rewards for genealogical information)
18. directories, lists, or other mention of genealogists, whether amateur or professional (such as lists of professional researchers available for hire)

19. names and addresses of genealogical and historical societies, family organizations, libraries, or archives (and sometimes titles of their publications)
20. articles or advertisements concerning genealogical seminars, workshops, and other instructional classes
21. accession lists, or articles describing the holdings or services of genealogical/historical societies or libraries
22. articles describing the functions of genealogical organizations
23. photographs of original documents or other records
24. individual or family photographs or portraits
25. corrections or additions to articles or material previously published in the particular magazine or published in another source
26. maps of states, counties, provinces, and other localities (historical, current, or outline maps)
27. letters to the editor
28. editorial articles or comments
29. reports of meetings of genealogical organizations
30. lists of members (and their addresses) of the genealogical organization which sponsors the magazine (especially lists of new members)
31. offers of free assistance to genealogists, or requests for information (such as "books wanted")
32. bibliographies or other lists of genealogical/historical sources, sometimes with descriptive notes
33. examples of forms used in notekeeping and recordkeeping, i.e., pedigree charts and family group record forms
34. records and sources pertaining to minorities

Genealogical periodicals tend to specialize in publishing specific types of articles, reflecting the editorial commitments of that publication, although these commitments may have changed over a period of time. It is, therefore, highly unlikely that a particular magazine will publish all or most of the above-mentioned items between its covers, nor would any one magazine have space to publish such information. The scope of genealogical periodicals is as varied as their titles imply. See appendix 3 for an extensive list of periodical titles and an indication of their scope.

LIMITATIONS OF PERIODICALS

There are a few limitations in the use of genealogical periodical literature; as printed sources the information in them needs to be used with some degree of reservation or skepticism. In fact, all printed sources need to be used with caution; the genealogist should not believe everything he reads in print. Derek Harland has stated, "It seems to be a common failing among beginning genealogists--although even the more experienced are often caught off guard--to accept anything of a genealogical nature merely because it is in print."[4] Printed secondary sources need to be carefully evaluated before accepting them as sources of genealogical information.

The quality of the genealogies and pedigrees published in periodicals depends upon two key factors: (1) who compiled the genealogy and the care with which the data were analyzed and related, and (2) the accuracy of the source or sources used in the compilation. In other words, some family histories and genealogies have been meticulously compiled while the accuracy of others is questionable. Because published family genealogies are compiled from other records, they are classified as printed secondary sources.

Verification of the data contained in periodical articles is advisable. This can be done by checking the sources used by the compiler, if documented in the article. In those genealogies that list the sources used in the compilation, the researcher ought to check original records. Even if little or no documentation is used in the periodical article, the information will still be of value, giving clues to names, dates, localities, and relationships which can then be verified by performing searches in original records and other sources. Some of these clues may not have been previously known.

There are other reasons for errors in periodical literature. These include printing errors and transcribing errors made when copying from original records. Even though genealogical periodicals are not a primary source, they have their rightful place in the genealogical research process.

TYPES OF GENEALOGICAL PERIODICALS

For purposes of this book, genealogical periodical literature may be conveniently classified into the following seven general categories:

I. INTERNATIONAL PERIODICALS

International genealogical periodicals publish articles and information of interest to those genealogists performing research in several different countries. These periodicals may concentrate on publishing articles and material pertaining to one country but may include occasional articles from many different countries, or they may attempt to publish a variety of articles from many different countries. Most of the articles published in international periodicals deal with record sources and research methodology.

II. NATIONAL PERIODICALS

National genealogical periodicals usually publish articles and sources pertaining to one particular country, but may include occasional articles concerning research or sources in other countries. Local and regional articles may also be within the scope of national periodicals.

III. REGIONAL PERIODICALS

Regional genealogical periodicals publish articles and genealogies concerned with a specific region within a country. In the United

States, this could be New England, the Middle Atlantic, the South, the Midwest, or the West. As differentiated from local periodicals, regional genealogical periodicals publish material concerning two or more states.

IV. LOCAL PERIODICALS

Local genealogical periodicals publish articles and source material relating to families and records of the state, province, or locality in which they are published; but they may also include occasional articles concerning families or records of neighboring states or other parts of the country. Local periodicals seldom publish articles concerning records or research in foreign countries. Often, each issue emphasizes records from one particular county or state.

V. FAMILY AND SURNAME PERIODICALS

Family newsletters and periodicals are published principally for the descendants of a common ancestor or for those interested in a particular surname, or several surnames. Family publications are often prepared by an established family organization. Some are mimeographed while others are printed using modern printing methods.

Surname magazines, unlike family magazines, do not restrict themselves to one or two specific pedigree lines, but usually publish genealogical information concerning individuals of a particular surname. These family names are often taken from one or several sources and may be published serially. Very often no attempt is made in surname periodicals to identify antecedents or descendants of individuals.

VI. ETHNIC PERIODICALS

These periodicals are published for a specific group having common interests, such as language, religion, culture, or race. They are often of limited circulation, highly specialized in nature, and their scope is somewhat confined to that particular group.

VII. SPECIALIZED SUBJECT PERIODICALS

Specialized subject periodicals publish information concerning a particular topic, such as heraldry or orders of chivalry. Or, they may offer specialized services, such as sales, rentals, or exchanges of genealogical materials. Other examples of this type of periodical are publications of patriotic and hereditary societies.

OTHER EXAMPLES OF PERIODICAL LITERATURE

Some genealogical periodicals specialize in publishing transcriptions from original records. One particularly fine example is TREE TALKS, published quarterly by the Central New York Genealogical Society. In addition to queries, news articles, and New York maps, this periodical publishes numerous abstracts and extracts from New York records, such as Bible records of New York families, vital and church records, court and probate records, military records, naturalizations, census records, cemetery records and tombstone inscriptions, civil records, newspapers, and other sources of interest to New York genealogists and those researching in the Middle Atlantic states.

Some genealogical periodicals publish articles which contain genealogical information peripheral to the state in which they are published, in addition to records from their own state or locality. These serials print pedigrees and record sources from neighboring states, and some include material from foreign countries. The titles of such periodicals are often deceptively localized.

An excellent example of a periodical which publishes a variety of articles concerning genealogies in several states in the United States and various Canadian provinces is THE DETROIT SOCIETY FOR GENEALOGICAL RESEARCH MAGAZINE (hereafter cited as DSGR MAGAZINE), published quarterly by the Detroit Society for Genealogical Research, Inc. To illustrate the scope of this publication, we shall list some selected titles of articles contained in volume 36 (1972-73). These titles show the variety of articles published in one volume of this serial:

"John Noble and Children of Yorkshire, England and Racine County, Wisconsin"

"Some Forebears and Descendants of Lewis Reno, Huguenot Immigrant to Virginia"

"A Question of the Identity of John Johnson of Lebanon, New London County, Connecticut"

"Abraham Dingman of Ohio and Miami County, Indiana"

"The Reverend Ebenezer Fairchild of New York State and Indiana"

"Samuel Babcock of Vermont, New York State, and Michigan"

"Elijah and Aurelia (Bigelow) Bigelow of Quebec and Michigan"

"William King, Sr., of New Salem, Massachusetts"

"Boarding Students at Freemont Seminary in Norristown, Pennsylvania"

"Hitt-Wamsley Cemetery in Sullivan County, New York"

"Phonecia Cemetery in Ulster County, New York"

"Genealogical Research in Upstate New York"

"Findley Cemetery in Wayne County, New York"

Also included in issues of the DSGR MAGAZINE are family records and Bible records, genealogical queries and answers to queries, book reviews, news notes, Michigan cemetery records, biographies of deceased members of DSGR, lists of new members of DSGR with their home address, lists of publications for sale by DSGR, reports of meetings of this society, recent acquisitions to the Burton Historical Collection of the Detroit Public Library, other feature articles, and indexes to each volume.

RECOMMENDED SERIAL TITLES

Professional genealogists and libraries with genealogical collections should sub-scribe to the most essential genealogical periodicals currently published. As a minimum, the following five titles should be in the collections of concerned American genealogists and genealogical libraries. These titles are a must for genealogical libraries in the United States, regardless of their size.[5]

THE AMERICAN GENEALOGIST
THE GENEALOGICAL HELPER
GENEALOGICAL JOURNAL
GENEALOGY
NATIONAL GENEALOGICAL SOCIETY QUARTERLY

In addition to these four titles, the genealogist or genealogical library should subscribe to the foremost genealogical or historical periodicals published in their own state or region. These are often published by statewide or local genea-logical and historical societies. The genealogist or genealogical library may also wish to subscribe to a few of the major family and surname magazines, since these offer a contribution to the genealogical literature.

Appendix 3 lists titles of the most important genealogical periodicals published in North America, excluding titles of family and surname magazines. If the serial is still in print, its current address is shown (as of 1977).

Several other professional journals are of interest to American genealogists. These occasionally publish articles and news notes of concern to genealogists. Two such scholarly journals are:

THE AMERICAN ARCHIVIST, published quarterly by the Society of American Archivists, 801 South Morgan, Chicago, Ill. 60680.

PROLOGUE: THE JOURNAL OF THE NATIONAL ARCHIVES, published quarterly by the National Archives, General Services Administration, Washington, D.C. 20408.

HISTORICAL PERIODICALS

Articles of interest to the genealogist can be found in some of the historical periodicals published in the United States, Canada, and in other countries. These are usually published by state and local historical societies and may con-tain data relating to the following:

1. biographical and historical information concerning early settlers and pioneers of a particular locality
2. pictures or portraits of individuals, buildings, towns, cemeteries, and other historical material
3. maps and sketches of localities
4. records of military regiments
5. local churches and their relationship to the community
6. local record sources and definitions
7. bibliographies
8. book reviews
9. other articles of a historical nature

Most historical periodicals will be of interest to the serious genealogist. The contents and scope of these publications vary in much the same way that the contents of genealogical periodicals vary.

CONCLUSION

Genealogical periodicals may be published by libraries, genealogical and historical societies, patriotic and hereditary societies, family organizations or associations, private individuals, and government agencies. The scope and value of these periodicals vary in both quality and quantity.[6]

The American genealogist is inundated with the growth of genealogical periodicals. These serials run the gamut from the scholarly genealogical journal written for the professional or the advanced amateur, to the one- or two-page mimeographed family newsletter. Countless genealogical periodicals have been published since the beginning of the twentieth century. Many have been short-lived. They are very often published quarterly, but many are issued monthly, bimonthly, semiannually, or annually. Appendix 3 classifies many current and retrospective American genealogical periodicals according to their scope, frequency of publication, and priority rating.

DEFINITIONS

Since the terms "periodical" and "serial" are often used interchangeably, the following definitions are offered by the American Library Association:

PERIODICAL: A publication with a distinctive title intended to appear in successive (usually unbound) numbers or parts at stated or regular intervals and, as a rule, for an indefinite time. Each part generally contains articles by several contributors. (Newspapers, whose chief function it is to disseminate news, and the memoirs, proceedings, journals, etc., of societies are not considered periodicals under the rules for cataloging.)

SERIAL: 1. A publication issued in successive parts, usually at regular intervals, and, as a rule, intended to be continued indefinitely. Serials include periodicals, annuals (reports, year-books, etc.), and memoirs, proceedings, and transactions of societies. 2. Any literary composition, especially a novel, published in consecutive numbers of a periodical.[7]

NOTES

1. Milton Rubincam, "Pitfalls in Genealogical Research," NATIONAL GENEALOGICAL SOCIETY QUARTERLY 43 (1955): 44-45.

2. Noel C. Stevenson, THE GENEALOGICAL READER (Salt Lake City: Deseret Book Co., 1958), p. v. Reprint, New Orleans: Polyanthos, 1977.

3. A "query" is a brief request for genealogical information. Refer to Chapter 9.

4. Derek Harland, GENEALOGICAL RESEARCH STANDARDS (Salt Lake City: Bookcraft, 1963), p. 352.

5. Refer to Appendix 3 for the mailing address of these titles. Other important American genealogical periodical titles are listed in appendix 3, along with a priority rating.

6. An interesting and somewhat related article is by Floren Stocks Preece, "The Value and Use of Genealogical Magazines," THE GENEALOGY CLUB OF AMERICA MAGAZINE 1 (1970): 8-10; reprinted in GENEALOGY DIGEST 7 (1976): 115-16.

7. Reprinted by permission from the American Library Association, Editorial Committee, Sub-committee on Library Terminology, ALA GLOSSARY OF LIBRARY TERMS, prepared by Elizabeth H. Thompson. Copyrighted 1943 and renewed 1971 by the American Library Association, Chicago. Other organizations offer similar definitions of these two terms.

Chapter 3

THE INDEX: ACCESS TO THE LITERATURE

An index is an indispensable tool for the genealogist and is the means by which a genealogist gains access to massive amounts of genealogical information. It is a guide to the text of reading matter and to the contents of collected material. A well-prepared index is invaluable as a time-saver and as a guide to finding references in a book or collection of records.

A comprehensive definition of an index is found in TRAINING IN INDEXING: A COURSE OF THE SOCIETY OF INDEXERS:

> A systematic guide to the text of any reading matter or to the contents of other collected documentary material, comprising a series of entries, with headings arranged in alphabetical or other chosen order and with references to show where each item indexed is located.[1]

Genealogical indexes contain surnames or complete personal names (surnames and given names), and some may include subject entries (topics) and localities (place names). Genealogical indexes may also index authors and titles of works, or portions of titles, although these entries are not as prevalent as in nongenealogical indexes.

Occasionally genealogical indexes show complete personal names followed by other identifying information, such as date of birth or name of spouse. This additional information is helpful in identifying the individual of interest. If an index contains only surnames, it is sometimes difficult to use when looking for common surnames such as Smith, Brown, or Jones.

Genealogical indexes are usually alphabetically arranged. This alphabetical arrangement has the advantage of saving a researcher the time it would otherwise take to search an original or printed record page by page and line by line.

Indexes to books, periodicals, and other printed sources sometimes have cross-references, such as "see" and "see also" references. These refer the reader from one heading or subheading to another. Cross-references are useful since two or more words may have nearly the same meaning. A "see" reference guides the reader to an alternative heading under which all relevant references to an item are listed. A "see also" reference directs the reader to additional headings under which further entries are to be found. Cross-references are more predominant in nongenealogical indexes, however.

Indexes can be found in a variety of formats, for example, card indexes, computerized indexes, microforms, printed indexes, typescript indexes, or manuscript indexes. This chapter focuses on published indexes, including indexes to genealogical periodicals, and attempts to show how genealogists may effectively use these tools in their research.

EFFECTIVE USE OF INDEXES

When using an index, the researcher is faced with the problem of determining its accuracy and completeness. A good approach is to select randomly a few names or topics from the work--if the work which was indexed is available to the researcher--and then determine how the names or topics were indexed, if at all. This procedure will give an indication of the completeness of the index and will show what reference system is used in the work. Some indexes refer the user to page numbers while others indicate sequential numbers in the work, a system often used in family histories and published genealogies. The researcher should also note the length of the index in proportion to the length of the original work.

With experience, the genealogist can make proper use of indexes. Intuition is an asset when using indexes as well as other genealogical and historical sources. W.I.B. Beveridge has stated, "No set rules can be followed in research. The investigator has to exercise his ingenuity, originality and judgment and take advantage of every useful stratagem."[2]

The following describes a systematic approach when searching indexes to genealogical records:

One of the first steps in genealogical research is to select a pedigree objective. For example, an objective might be to locate the parents of a given ancestor, or to identify a particular date and place of marriage. Next determine which indexes and records might contain relevant information to help reach or solve the selected objective. Deciding which indexes might assist in solving a research problem requires an understanding of basic research principles and a knowledge of record sources.

The next step is to determine where the pertinent indexes and genealogical sources are housed. Locating these sources depends upon which libraries and record repositories the researcher has access to. Correspondence with other libraries and repositories may be needed in order to locate sources which have been found in an index.

After locating the index of interest, the preface or introduction to the index should be read before beginning a search for names or topics. The introductory portion of a work or index may define the scope and limitations of the index and may indicate any indexing peculiarities, abbreviations, or symbols used in the index or in the work itself.

Understanding the arrangement of the index is an important initial step when using an index, since indexes are not all arranged the same. Some indexes are divided by personal names and may have a separate listing of localities or subjects, while others have names and topics in one alphabetic sequence.

The genealogist will need to search all available indexes to the work or collection of interest in order to exhaust the access tools to that particular source. A genealogist who has a healthy curiosity will examine all relevant indexes to a record or collection.

It is wise to check all possible spelling variations when using an index. The user of the index does not always know the contents of the original source nor would he know how the indexer interpreted the entries. Substituting one vowel for another will sometimes change a name considerably. Variants of a word or surname may be cross-referenced or may be shown in parentheses in the index.

Each index searched should be carefully scrutinized for all possible references to the family of interest. This approach is particularly helpful if the genealogist is searching an index for common names. When searching an index for a particular person, also check for the name of the spouse, names of parents, names of children, and names of other close family members. Maiden names of married women should be checked as well.

When using an index, one should check to see if it has an addenda, corrections, or some similar section. Some indexes contain additions and corrections which may be located at the end of the index, or placed somewhere else in the work. The name of interest could have been overlooked initially but may have been found and placed in an addendum. The researcher should also determine if names or other entries were printed out of alphabetical order in the index since all indexes are not strictly alphabetical.

If an entry of interest is located in an index, the researcher should copy all the data shown for that entry, such as name, page number, volume number, date, locality, or other reference. It may be wise to reproduce that particular index page using a photocopy machine. Armed with this information, the researcher is then able to begin a search for the source indexed. This could be a printed source, or an original record. The source may be available at the same library as the index or it may be at another repository. Some sources, or photocopies of records, may be obtained from a library through interlibrary loan.

After locating an entry in an index or transcription, it is advisable to attempt to locate and read the original source. Not only is the original source more accurate, but one may be able to find additional data in the original which were not recorded in the index or abstract. The source indexed could be a printed secondary source, such as a family history or periodical, or it could be a primary source, such as a church register or court record.

When the source indexed is located, the researcher should then match the reference(s) found in the index with those in the original. These references are usually page numbers; but they could also include volume numbers, district numbers, etc., depending upon the particular source which was indexed.

One caution in using indexes: they often refer the user to a page number for a particular name without indicating how many times that name appears on the page--although some indexes do give this indication. One should always scan the entire page in the work for more than one reference to the name or subject of interest. In fact, it might be wise to read a few pages before and after the referenced page. This not only may reveal information omitted from the index, but will often help place the desired information in proper perspective.

Indexes to special collections and to the genealogical literature can be used as finding tools in order to discover lost ancestors or persons for whom no former city and/or state of residence is known. Indexes can be used to pinpoint a name in a particular state or locality during a given period of time. This is particularly true of indexes to both statewide and local censuses, indexes to land and military records, and indexes to local histories. There are other indexes on a federal, state, and local basis. Indexes to family histories and indexes to genealogical periodicals can also be valuable tools.[3]

The genealogist often turns to such locator sources when attempting to identify a family name in a particular locality. Locator sources are used when the genealogist is uncertain of a place of residence of an ancestor. Once a specific locality is discovered, county and other local records can then be searched for the ancestral objective.

LIMITATIONS OF INDEXES

Indexes are a secondary source and, as such, should be used with some reservation. The genealogist must realize there is always a chance for errors or omissions in an index. These might include copying errors on the part of the indexer, or the indexer may have omitted an entry entirely. It is not uncommon for the researcher to find printing errors in an index. Few indexes are perfect and many are incomplete. Some indexes are more meticulously prepared than others.

An index guides the researcher to secondary and primary sources. Like printed family histories and other secondary sources, indexes must be used carefully.

Used correctly, however, an index is helpful in directing the researcher to valuable information which may eventually solve a pedigree problem. In order to utilize an index effectively, the user must determine the depth of the index. The quality of the index often depends a great deal upon its compiler and publisher.

The user of an index does not always know how the entry was spelled in the original record. Unless variant spellings are checked, the researcher may overlook the entry because of its particular spelling or alphabetical arrangement in the index. Cross-references can be found in some genealogical indexes.

Women's names could be indexed under one of several different surnames, or not indexed at all. When searching for a woman's name in an index, one ought to look under both her married surname and maiden name since she could be listed under either name or both names. The maiden surname of a married woman may be shown in parentheses, thereby giving additional aid to the researcher. Unfortunately, women's names are often excluded from indexes, making them more elusive than men's names.

Modern indexes are often more thorough than most of the indexes published in earlier years, such as nineteenth-century indexes. Current published works often contain every-name indexes, whereas older publications are likely to contain indexes only to the most significant or principal individuals mentioned in a work or in biographical sketches, or to names deemed relevant by the indexer. This is true for many local histories and collected local biographies.

Some or all of these limitations could apply to indexes to genealogical periodical literature. Indexes to this literature are by no means comprehensive. Usually only the principal person or surname from a periodical article is included in composite genealogical periodical indexes; often only the immigrant ancestor is indexed. An important consideration in using these indexes is that there is no comprehensive index to all major genealogical periodicals published in the United States and Canada.

USING GENEALOGICAL PERIODICAL INDEXES

To use indexes to genealogical periodical literature effectively, the researcher should first select a pedigree objective, making particular note of pertinent names, dates, and places of important genealogical events such as birth, marriage, residence, and death. One should then search for the selected surname, or, depending upon the periodical index, the complete personal name, in periodical indexes. These indexes will be further defined in subsequent chapters in this book. Spelling variations should not be overlooked.

The researcher should next search the periodical indexes under the specific locality where the ancestor of interest resided, was born, married, or died. References to printed locality records can be found by such an approach. Although the ancestor's name may not be listed in a periodical index, the person's name could very well be in printed records, such as births or marriages abstracted in a periodical.

Some periodical indexes use the "indirect locality" approach, listing materials by state and thereunder alphabetically by county. The following are examples of indirect locality headings:

NEW YORK, ALBANY COUNTY
OHIO, GEAUGA COUNTY
PENNSYLVANIA, ALLEGHENY COUNTY

Smaller localities and the type of record indexed are sometimes shown alphabetically following the name of the county.

Other periodical indexes use the "direct locality" approach, listing the smallest jurisdiction first, such as the name of the town or county. The following are examples of direct locality entries:

ALBANY, ALBANY COUNTY, NEW YORK
CHARDON, GEAUGA COUNTY, OHIO
PITTSBURGH, ALLEGHENY COUNTY, PENNSYLVANIA

Additional locality information might be found in a periodical index under the name of the country or region, such as New England. Printed sources may also be listed in the periodical index under a general subject (topical) heading. A few selected examples of subject headings used in some periodical indexes are the following:

AMERICAN INDIAN GENEALOGY
HERALDRY
LOYALISTS
METHODOLOGY
NAMES

Events may also be indexed, such as Revolutionary War, or Civil War.

The mass of genealogical periodical literature can most effectively be searched by first checking a composite periodical index--one which indexes two or more periodical titles. Many hours of research could be saved if genealogists would make use of the composite periodical indexes discussed later in this book.

The advantages of searching composite indexes to genealogical periodicals are twofold: (1) these indexes bring together a variety of entries from periodicals in one volume, in one or more alphabetic arrangements; (2) the genealogist can search these indexes for one or more pedigree objectives without knowing exact locality references.

In addition to the composite indexes described in the following chapters, there are other periodical indexes, such as those bound with each individual serial, as well as other specialized indexes to published sources of interest to genealogists.

The genealogical researcher must be imaginative when searching periodical indexes. Subject headings are not consistent among the various American periodical indexes. Indexing techniques are likewise not consistent among these indexes.

Each periodical index has its unique arrangement, scope, and depth of indexing. Modern periodical indexes usually index complete personal names, subjects, and localities, whereas older indexes index only surnames.

Annual or cumulative indexes may be bound with the periodical, or they may be published separately. Annual indexes to serials often appear with the final yearly issue which is often published in December. These annual indexes may be later combined into cumulative indexes to that particular serial title. It is encouraging to see cumulative periodical indexes, as these simplify the researcher's problem of access to the genealogical literature.

SUPPLEMENTARY READINGS

The following selected bibliography contains titles of periodical articles and books concerning the subject of indexing. These references will be of particular interest to genealogists, historians, indexers, and genealogical librarians. Various indexing methods, and approaches to the use of indexes, are described in these sources. Some of these references have bibliographies which will direct the reader to other materials on the subject of genealogical and historical indexing.

"Alternate Name Spelling, Pitfall of Indexing." TRI-STATE TRADER, 28 August 1976, p. 45.

"An Index to Indexes." GENEALOGY DIGEST 6 (1975): 17.

Askling, John. "Confusion Worse Confounded: How to Evaluate an Index." CALIFORNIA LIBRARIAN 13 (1951): 3.

Boykin, Lucile A. "Indexes to Genealogy Magazines." THE QUARTERLY 16 (1970): 19-21.

Brahm, Walter. PUBLISHING GENEALOGICAL INDEXES, PART II, HOW THE 1820 AND 1830 CENSUSES OF OHIO WERE INDEXED. Area L-3b. World Conference on Records and Genealogical Seminar. Salt Lake City. 1969.

Claudia, Sister M. "Automated Techniques in Comprehensive Indexing." THE AMERICAN ARCHIVIST 30 (1967): 287-94.

Collison, Robert L. INDEXES AND INDEXING. 4th rev. ed. New York: DeGraff, 1972.

_____. INDEXING BOOKS: A MANUAL OF BASIC PRINCIPLES. New York: DeGraff, 1962.

Costley, Roberta H. "Suggestions on How to Index Your Genealogical Records." THE GENEALOGICAL RECORD 15 (1973): 47-49.

Everton, George B., Jr. PUBLISHING GENEALOGICAL INDEXES, PART I, THE PUBLISHING OF INDEXES BY MANUAL METHODS. Area L-3a. World Conference on Records and Genealogical Seminar. Salt Lake City. 1969.

Fish, Edwin N. "Indexing: Key to Genealogy Research." GENEALOGY DIGEST 5 (1974): 28.

Friedman, Harry A. NEWSPAPER INDEXING. Milwaukee: Marquette University Press, 1942; Ann Arbor, Mich.: University Microfilms, 1972.

Gates, Susa Young. "The Index as an Aid to the Genealogist." THE UTAH GENEALOGICAL AND HISTORICAL MAGAZINE 4 (1913): 130-33.

"Genealogical Research Notes: Tricks in Using Genealogical Books." GENEALOGICAL RESEARCH NEWS 6 (1968): 1.

Heiss, Willard. "Consider the Index." GENEALOGY, no. 10 (1974), pp. 1-17. Reprinted from THE COUNTY COURTHOUSES AND RECORDS OF MARYLAND, PART TWO: THE RECORDS, pp. 20-36. Publication no. 13. Annapolis, Md.: Hall of Records Commission, 1963.

Hunnisett, R. F. INDEXING FOR EDITORS. Cambridge: British Records Association, 1972.

THE INDEXER. London: Society of Indexers, 1958-- . Biannual.

"INDEXES." In A MANUAL OF STYLE, 12th ed., rev. Chicago: University of Chicago Press, 1969.

Ireland, Norma Olin. "Genealogical Indexes 'Simplify' Searching." TRI-STATE TRADER, 30 October 1976, p. 45.

_____. "Genealogical Indexing: 'Tips' for the Amateur." TRI-STATE TRAD-ER, 2 October 1976, p. 45.

_____. "Lesser-Known Indexes Noted as Aids for Genealogists." TRI-STATE TRADER, 13 November 1976, p. 45.

_____. "Maternal Lines Sometimes Neglected in Indexing." TRI-STATE TRAD-ER, 16 October 1976, p. 45.

_____. "Name Variants, Omissions, Problem for Indexer." TRI-STATE TRAD-ER, 9 October 1976, pp. 45-46.

_____. "Some Cemetery, Church Records Compiled but Not Printed." TRI-STATE TRADER, 6 November 1976, pp. 45-46.

_____. "So, You're Going to 'Make an Index'!" THE COLONIAL GENEA-LOGIST 7 (1974-75): 694-97, 921-23, 1001-3.

Jacobus, Donald Lines. "Hints on Indexing." THE AMERICAN GENEALOGIST 34 (1958): 89-94. Reprinted in BULLETIN OF THE STAMFORD GENEALOGI-CAL SOCIETY 7 (1965): 47-51.

_____. "Tricks in Using Indexed Genealogical Books." THE AMERICAN GENEALOGIST 30 (1954): 85-89. Reprinted in Noel C. Stevenson's THE GENEALOGICAL READER, Salt Lake City: Deseret Book Co., 1958.

Jillson, Willard Rouse. "The Indexing of Historical Materials." THE AMERI-CAN ARCHIVIST 16 (1953): 251-57.

Josephson, Bertha E. "Indexing." THE AMERICAN ARCHIVIST 10 (1947): 133-50.

Karns, Kermit B. "Indexing Genealogical Information." THE KANSAS CITY GENEALOGIST 3 (1963): 15-16.

Kirkham, E. Kay. "Did You Say That You 'Checked' the Index?" GENEA-LOGICAL JOURNAL 1 (1972): 26-27.

Knight, G. Norman, ed. TRAINING IN INDEXING: A COURSE OF THE SOCIETY OF INDEXERS. Cambridge, Mass.: M.I.I. Press, 1969.

Management Information Services. STUDIES IN INDEXING AND CATALOG-ING. Detroit: Management Information Services, n.d.

Marsh, Warren L. SEARCH AND RETRIEVAL: THE APPLICATION OF DATA
PROCESSING TO GENEALOGICAL RESEARCH. Old Saybrook, Conn.: Published by the author, 1970.

Mayhill, R.T. "Census Indexes Useful but Can Be Misleading." TRI-STATE
TRADER, 30 March 1974, pp. 36-37.

_____. "Even More Indexes Needed; Information Can Be Coded." TRI-
STATE TRADER, 24 August 1974, p. 38.

_____. "Have a Yen for Indexing Old Deeds?--Some Suggestions." TRI-
STATE TRADER, 23 March 1974, pp. 36-37.

_____. "Index: The Genealogist's Most Useful Tool." TRI-STATE TRADER,
27 December 1975, pp. 29-30.

_____. "Indexing of Newspapers is Worthy Project." TRI-STATE TRADER,
1 February 1975, p. 30.

_____. "Is Fairfax Co., Va., Project Prelude to More Indexing?" TRI-
STATE TRADER, 13 March 1976, p. 44.

Metcalfe, John Wallace. SUBJECT CLASSIFYING AND INDEXING OF LI-
BRARIES AND LITERATURE. New York: Scarecrow Press, 1959.

Montgomery, Austin H., Jr. "Speeding Indexing of Genealogical Data by
Computer." NATIONAL GENEALOGICAL SOCIETY QUARTERLY 64 (1976):
35-44.

Moran, Abby. "Genealogical Indexing." STIRPES 6 (1966): 123-31.

Neiman, Stella Duff, and Cappon, Lester J. "Comprehensive Historical Indexing: The Virginia Gazette Index." THE AMERICAN ARCHIVIST 14 (1951):
291-304.

Preece, Floren Stocks. "The Value and Use of Genealogical Magazines."
THE GENEALOGY CLUB OF AMERICA MAGAZINE 1 (1970): 8-10; reprinted
in GENEALOGY DIGEST 7 (1976): 115-16.

Prindle, Paul W. "Indexing Comments." BULLETIN OF THE STAMFORD
GENEALOGICAL SOCIETY 7 (1965): 51-54.

Radoff, Morris L.; Skordas, Gust; and Jacobsen, Phebe R. THE COUNTY
COURTHOUSES AND RECORDS OF MARYLAND, PART TWO: THE RECORDS.
Publication no. 13. Annapolis, Md.: Hall of Records Commission, 1963.

"Random Thoughts on Indexing." THE AMERICAN GENEALOGIST 50 (1974): inside back cover.

Skillin, Marjorie E., and Gay, Robert M. WORDS INTO TYPE. 3d ed., rev. Englewood Cliffs, N.J.: Prentice-Hall, 1974.

Smith, Russell M. "Item Indexing by Automated Processes." THE AMERICAN ARCHIVIST 30 (1967): 295-302.

Sperry, Kip. "The Index: A Tool for the Genealogist." THE GENEALOGICAL HELPER 30 (1976): 10-12.

_____. "A Study of Bibliographical Control of United States Genealogical Periodical Literature." Master's project, Brigham Young University, Provo, Utah, 1974. Unpublished.

Sperry, Kip, and Scanland, Roger. "Searching the Genealogical Literature: Periodical Indexes." NATIONAL GENEALOGICAL SOCIETY QUARTERLY 63 (1975): 186-93.

Sprenger, Bernice. "The Indispensable Index." THE DETROIT SOCIETY FOR GENEALOGICAL RESEARCH MAGAZINE 25 (1962): 139.

Towle, Laird C. GENEALOGICAL PERIODICALS: A NEGLECTED TREASURE. Bowie, Md.: Yankee Bookmen, 1977.

United States of America Standards Institute. USA STANDARD BASIC CRITERIA FOR INDEXES. New York: 1969. Formerly American Standards Association, AMERICAN STANDARD BASIC CRITERIA FOR INDEXES, New York, 1959.

Vallentine, John F. "Effective Use of Census Indexes in Locating People." GENEALOGICAL JOURNAL 4 (1975): 51-60.

_____. LOCALITY FINDING AIDS FOR U.S. SURNAMES. Logan, Utah: Everton Publishers, 1975.

Walrath, Arthur J. COUNTY COURTHOUSE RECORDS: A BASIC SOURCE OF DATA. Agricultural Experiment Station, Blacksburg, Virginia, Bulletin no. 560. Blacksburg, Va.: 1965.

Walsh, John W.T. THE INDEXING OF BOOKS AND PERIODICALS. New York: R.R. Bowker, 1931.

Wheeler, Martha Thorne. INDEXING: PRINCIPLES, RULES AND EXAMPLES. 5th ed. New York (State) University, Bulletin no. 1445. Albany: New

York State Library, University of the State of New York, 1957.

Wood, Ralph V., Jr. "The Census Index Problem." NATIONAL GENEALOGI-
CAL SOCIETY QUARTERLY 56 (1968): 188-92.

NOTES

1. G. Norman Knight, ed., TRAINING IN INDEXING: A COURSE OF THE
SOCIETY OF INDEXERS (Cambridge, Mass.: M.I.T. Press, 1969), p. 10.

2. W.I.B. Beveridge, THE ART OF SCIENTIFIC INVESTIGATION, 3d ed.
(New York: Vintage Books, 1957), p. 175.

3. There are other specialized locator sources used in American research. A
particularly fine example is THE AMERICAN GENEALOGICAL-BIOGRAPHICAL
INDEX (Middletown, Conn.: Godfrey Memorial Library, 1952--).

Chapter 4

THE MUNSELL INDEXES

The first significant attempt to index American printed sources including genealogical periodicals was published by the Joel Munsell publishers of Albany,
New York. Initially appearing in 1868 and edited by Daniel Steele Durrie,
this index appeared under the rather grandiose title, BIBLIOGRAPHIA GENEA-
LOGICA AMERICANA: AN ALPHABETICAL INDEX TO AMERICAN GENEA-
LOGIES AND PEDIGREES CONTAINED IN STATE, COUNTY AND TOWN
HISTORIES, PRINTED GENEALOGIES, AND KINDRED WORKS. It contained
about 10,000 alphabetized surname references. Revised and enlarged editions
were published in 1878 (2d edition) and 1886 (3d edition).

After Durrie died, the Munsell firm assumed editorship and the title was changed
in the fourth edition of 1895 to the INDEX TO AMERICAN GENEALOGIES;
AND TO GENEALOGICAL MATERIAL CONTAINED IN ALL WORKS, SUCH
AS TOWN HISTORIES, COUNTY HISTORIES, LOCAL HISTORIES, HISTORICAL
SOCIETY PUBLICATIONS, BIOGRAPHIES, HISTORICAL PERIODICALS, AND
KINDRED WORKS. The lengthy subtitle is not generally used by genealogists.

Most American genealogists are familiar with the fifth edition of INDEX TO
AMERICAN GENEALOGIES, which carried the same subtitle as the fourth edition. The fifth edition, published in 1900, contains 352 pages and has nearly
50,000 entries. It includes all of the entries found in the earlier editions.
The fifth revised edition is the most popular of the Munsell indexes, and has
been reprinted by Gale Research Company of Detroit (1966) and by Genealogical Publishing Company of Baltimore (1967).

In 1908 the Munsell firm published SUPPLEMENT 1900 TO 1908 TO THE IN-
DEX TO GENEALOGIES PUBLISHED IN 1900, which has also been reprinted
by Gale Research and Genealogical Publishing. The SUPPLEMENT has approximately 10,000 entries in its 107 pages; it is published in the reprint editions
of INDEX TO AMERICAN GENEALOGIES. The title is somewhat misleading,
it includes entries from some books and periodicals published prior to 1900 which
were not included in the 1900 index. The majority of the entries are from
genealogical publications which were published between 1900 and 1908. The
format of the SUPPLEMENT is identical to that of its predecessor, INDEX TO
AMERICAN GENEALOGIES. The SUPPLEMENT and the 1900 INDEX need to
be searched together in order to use this source effectively.

The Munsell Indexes

Both the INDEX TO AMERICAN GENEALOGIES and its SUPPLEMENT 1900 TO 1908 index a considerable number of American genealogical periodicals, family and local histories, and similar printed sources. A few newspaper genealogy columns have also been partially indexed. These two indexes contain a representative number of entries for the New England states and Middle Atlantic states but also include entries from southern and midwestern titles. The southern states are better represented in the SUPPLEMENT than in the INDEX TO AMERICAN GENEALOGIES.

Genealogical periodicals and family histories were not, to any great extent, published west of the Mississippi River prior to 1900 and thus are not represented in Munsell's indexes. In a study of the Munsell indexes, Roger Scanland observed, "The Munsell index does make a serious omission, however, in failing to cover county and local histories published west of the Mississippi."[1] Few references to Canadian publications can be found in these two Munsell indexes.

A major limitation in using these two indexes is that both are surname indexes only. Also, no attempt was made to include all surnames from a given work. Only prominent surnames which were dealt with at length are included. The preface indicates, "In most cases the references are to matter which consists of at least three or four generations." Family histories are represented only by the principal surname in the history.

Although the Munsell indexes are not comprehensive in their indexing, they are important surname indexes to numerous American printed sources. These indexes have contributed a great deal to the genealogical literature. They contain thousands of surname references from works published prior to 1908 and are therefore valuable genealogical indexes and reference sources. These indexes should be available at most libraries in the United States which have a genealogical collection.

The surnames indexed in these two works are shown in bold (black) type followed by an alphabetical listing of authors and shortened titles where that surname appears. Some representative entries from INDEX TO AMERICAN GENEALOGIES are presented in Figure 1. As can be seen by this example, Munsell used an abbreviated style of citation for the majority of the author and title entries. The concise citation refers to the title of the book or periodical; the author's surname is shown along with the book's volume and page numbers (and sometimes the year published). Volume numbers are shown in lowercase roman numerals. Inclusive page numbers are shown in most of the citations.

The shortened citations may present some difficulties in locating the source indexed in a library's card catalog or in a bibliography. A listing of sources indexed is not included in the Munsell publications; neither is there an explanation of the abbreviations used in their index references. An additional problem is Munsell's occasional reference to the same title in several different ways.

Cornish — Davis' Landmarks 70-2
Hinman's Connecticut Settlers 722-4
Savage's Genealogical Dictionary i, 458
Cornu — Stearns' Ashburnham 655
Cornwall — Andrews' New Britain 229
Goodwin's Foote Genealogy 245
Hall's Genealogical Notes (1886) 152
Hinman's Connecticut Settlers 724
New Eng. Hist. and Gen. Reg. xlix, 39-45
Cornwallis — Neill's Carolorum 99
Cornwell — American Ancestry ii, 28
Coe and Ward Memorial 52-5
Kellogg's White Genealogy 27
Middlefield Ct. History
Savage's Genealogical Dictionary i, 459
Corp — Austin's R. I. Gen. Dictionary 56
Corr — Clarke's King Wm. Va. Fams.
Correll — Power's Sangamon 228-30
Corse — Morris Genealogy (1898) 629
Sheldon's Deerfield 133-6, 388
Temple's Northfield Mass. 425
Corsen — Clute's Staten Island 358-62
Corser — American Ancestry x, 43
Coffin's History of Boscawen N. H. 497-509
Corson — American Ancestry, ix, 163
Davis' History of Bucks County Pa. 357
Dearborn's History of Salisbury N. H. 531
Neff Genealogy 316
Corss — American Ancestry ix, 54
Corteis — Barry's Hanover 272-88
Cortelyou —Bergen Genealogy 90, 128, 150
Bergen's Kings Co. N. Y. Settlers 74-6
Clute's History of Staten Island N. Y. 363
Honeyman's Our Home Magazine 242
Nevius Genealogy
Van Brunt Genealogy 18
Corthell — Barry's Hanover Mass. 271
Hobart's History of Abington Mass. 365
Lincoln's History of Hingham Mass. ii,
    140-4
Whitman Genealogy 141

Fig. 1

Example from INDEX TO AMERICAN GENEALOGIES

The following two procedures will be helpful in locating the complete bibliographic references from the abbreviated citation used by Munsell:

1. Family history entries (such as Walworth's HYDE GENEALOGY) should first be checked in THE AMERICAN GENEALOGIST, 5th edition.[2] This latter work is discussed later in this chapter. This work contains the complete title and author for each family history listed in these Munsell indexes. After obtaining this information, the researcher should be able to locate the desired item in a library card catalog or bibliography. One may also wish to check the three-volume work, GENEALOGIES IN THE LIBRARY OF CONGRESS: A BIBLIOGRAPHY,[3] to locate the full name of authors and titles of many family histories.

2. Local history entries (such as Temple's HISTORY OF PALMER, MASS.) may be located in a card catalog by checking under the headings "History" or "Genealogy" in the appropriate locality section. An alternative procedure would be to search for the author's name in the card catalog of authors. This latter approach is less practical unless the author's surname is uncommon. However, authors' full names can often be obtained by checking UNITED STATES LOCAL HISTORIES IN THE LIBRARY OF CONGRESS.[4] The researcher may also find the local history of interest by browsing through the shelves in a genealogical library which has open stacks.

The intricacies involved in locating these abbreviated citations in a library card catalog or bibliography are apparent. The approaches which can be used in locating materials in most library card catalogs are (1) author, (2) title, (3) subject, and (4) locality (place names). Periodical titles may be listed in a card catalog by title, or they may be shown in a serials listing or other bibliography. Many libraries, particularly academic libraries, have computer printouts of their serial titles.

Even though there are numerous index entries for common surnames, the locality from the source indexed is sometimes shown in the Munsell citation. This will assist the researcher in determining if a surname can be found in a given locality and can at least narrow the research to a particular state or region. Some "see" references for surnames are used by Munsell, referring the reader from one spelling of a surname to another surname.

SERIALS INDEXED IN "INDEX TO AMERICAN GENEALOGIES" AND ITS "SUPPLEMENT"

A listing of many of the titles which are partially indexed in INDEX TO AMERICAN GENEALOGIES and the SUPPLEMENT 1900 TO 1908 is shown below. No attempt has been made to verify the accuracy of each title cited. An effort has been made to show the most prominent titles indexed by Munsell in these two indexes from the frequency of listing in this work.

AMERICAN HISTORICAL REGISTER
AMERICAN HISTORY MAGAZINE
BALTIMORE SUN
BANGOR MAINE HISTORICAL MAGAZINE
BELLOWS FALLS TIMES
Burlington, County, New Jersey, DEMOCRAT
Charleston, S.C., NEWS
DEDHAM HISTORICAL REGISTER
Dover, New Hampshire, ENQUIRER
Doylestown, Pennsylvania, INTELLIGENCER
ESSEX INSTITUTE HISTORICAL COLLECTIONS
ESSEX ANTIQUARIAN
Fernald's GENEALOGICAL EXCHANGE
GULF STATES HISTORICAL MAGAZINE
JERSEYMAN
Kewaunee, Wisconsin, OWL
KITTOCHTINNY MAGAZINE
KNOX COUNTY MAINE HISTORICAL MAGAZINE
MCCLURE'S MAGAZINE
MAGAZINE OF AMERICAN HISTORY
MAINE GENEALOGIST
MAINE HISTORICAL AND GENEALOGICAL RECORDER
MARYLAND HISTORICAL MAGAZINE
MASSACHUSETTS MAGAZINE
MAYFLOWER DESCENDANT
NARRAGANSETT HISTORICAL REGISTER
Needham, Massachusetts, GAZETTE
Newburgh, New York, TELEGRAM
NEW ENGLAND HISTORICAL AND GENEALOGICAL REGISTER
NEW ENGLAND MAGAZINE OF HISTORY
NEW JERSEY HISTORICAL SOCIETY PROCEEDINGS
New Paltz, N.Y., INDEPENDENT
NEWPORT HISTORY MAGAZINE
NEW YORK GENEALOGICAL AND BIOGRAPHICAL RECORD
Old Eliot, Maine, MAGAZINE
OLD NORTHWEST GENEALOGICAL QUARTERLY
ONTARIO HISTORICAL SOCIETY PAPERS
PERKIOMEN REGION (Pennsylvania)
PENNSYLVANIA GERMAN
PENNSYLVANIA MAGAZINE OF HISTORY
PUTNAM'S HISTORICAL MAGAZINE
QUINBY'S NEW ENGLAND FAMILY HISTORY QUARTERLY
Richmond, Virginia, TIMES
SOUTH CAROLINA HISTORICAL AND GENEALOGICAL MAGAZINE
SOUTHERN HISTORICAL ASSOCIATION PUBLICATIONS
TILLEY'S MAGAZINE OF NEW ENGLAND HISTORY
VIRGINIA MAGAZINE OF HISTORY
Washington, D. C., HISTORICAL BULLETIN
WEST VIRGINIA HISTORICAL MAGAZINE
WHITMORE'S HERALDIC JOURNAL
WILLIAM AND MARY COLLEGE QUARTERLY

MUNSELL'S GENEALOGICAL INDEX

In 1933, Joel Munsell's Sons published MUNSELL'S GENEALOGICAL INDEX
(South Norwalk, Conn.: Joel Munsell's Sons, 1933), which carried a lengthy
subtitle, AN INDEX TO GENEALOGICAL MATERIAL CONTAINED IN WORKS
SUCH AS TOWN HISTORIES, COUNTY HISTORIES, LOCAL HISTORIES, HIS-
TORICAL SOCIETY PUBLICATIONS, BIOGRAPHIES, HISTORICAL PERIODICALS,
GENEALOGIES AND KINDRED WORKS. Following the format of Munsell's
earlier indexes, only surnames are indexed; these are listed alphabetically followed by an abbreviated citation. MUNSELL'S GENEALOGICAL INDEX was
intended to update their INDEX TO AMERICAN GENEALOGIES; however, only
part one was published. Once again, no attempt was made to index all surnames in a given work. The preface to this index concisely defines its scope:

> This work, prepared with a view to facilitate the study of family
> history, indexes genealogical materials, by giving the titles of
> works containing references to genealogies of American Families,
> arranging the references alphabetically under family names. In
> most cases the references are to matter which consists of at least
> three or four generations.
>
> The surname is given in black type followed by the title or titles
> of works containing information on each surname, with number of
> the page or pages on which the information is to be found. Look
> for the various spellings of the name.
>
> References to town histories give the Author's name followed by the
> name of the town and State. References to periodicals give the
> name of the periodical, followed by the volume number, or date
> of issue.
>
> Family genealogies are listed under the family name, followed by
> the date of publication and the number of pages contained therein.
> These titles are given briefly each occupying one line in general.

Following the format of the SUPPLEMENT 1900 TO 1908, MUNSELL'S GENEA-
LOGICAL INDEX includes some entries from works published prior to 1900.
However, most entries are from histories, and genealogical and historical periodicals published between 1900 and 1932. Unfortunately, only the surnames
"Abbe" through "Dymont" are indexed in this forty-page work, the only volume
published by Munsell with this title. It contains about 2,900 entries. An
example from this particular index is shown in Figure 2.

LIST OF TITLES

Another important book by Munsell which partially indexes genealogical periodicals is entitled LIST OF TITLES OF GENEALOGICAL ARTICLES IN AMERICAN
PERIODICALS AND KINDRED WORKS (Albany, N.Y.: Joel Munsell's Sons,
1899). The title page further describes the work as "giving the name, residence, and earliest date of the first settler of each family, and adding deficiencies in brackets." This work is designed as a companion volume to THE
AMERICAN GENEALOGIST (see below).

Alden
Alden Fam. Mag. (1921)
Alden Genealogy (1909), 84 p.
Alden Kindred (1902), 8 p.
Ayer Ancestors (1905)
Dau. of the Rev. Mag., ii, 35-7
Flag Genealogy (1903)
Geneal. Mag., v, 429-35
Hayford Genealogy, 124-9
John Mellen's Sermon (1797)
Johnson Memorial (1905)
Lines of Desc. N. E. Ancestors (1897)
Mayflower Descendants ix, 145-51;x, 76-
    83; xi, 72-5; 140-2
McNair Ancestry (1912)
Munsey-Hopkins Genealogy (1920)
N. E. Fams. (1913), 217-9; 325-8; 496
N. Y. Gen. and Biog. Rec. xlix, 311-2
Alderman
Wakeman Genealogy (1900)
Aldis
Adis Genealogy (1914), 11 p.
Aldrich
Aldrich Genealogy (1911), 20
Comstock Genealogy (1905)
Frost Genealogy (1912)
Lakefort, N. H. Homes, 76-84
Mowry Genealogy (1909)
New England Fams. 1913)
Old. N. W. Gen. Quar., xii, (1909), 55-60

Fig. 2
Example from MUNSELL'S GENEALOGICAL INDEX

Containing approximately 1,450 entries, LIST OF TITLES gives titles of works with surnames, listed alphabetically by surname, which are shown in capital letters. Descriptions of the entry are placed in brackets and volume number, year, and page numbers are given. The surnames have been taken from titles of books and articles. The author of the work is sometimes included in the entry. The LIST OF TITLES contains 165 pages. An example is shown in Figure 3.

THE AMERICAN GENEALOGIST

THE AMERICAN GENEALOGIST: BEING A CATALOGUE OF FAMILY HISTORIES is an alphabetical listing of title pages taken from American family histories published in book and pamphlet form. The title page further states that this is "a bibliography of American genealogy or a list of the title pages of books and pamphlets on family history, published in America, from 1771 to date." The entries are listed by the major surname in the work; the surname is shown in capital letters. The first edition was issued in 1862, the second in 1886, the third in 1875, the fourth in 1897, and the fifth in 1900. As stated in the preface to the fifth edition, "The plan of the work is to give the title page of each book published on the genealogy of an American family, and the number of pages, together with other information."

The 1900 edition contains about 2,800 titles. No further description will be given here since this work is not an index to genealogical periodicals. This work has been mentioned since it can be a useful reference source, especially when used in conjunction with the Munsell indexes cited earlier in this chapter.

NOTES

1. Roger Scanland, "The Munsell Genealogical Indexes," GENEALOGICAL JOURNAL 2 (1973): 106. The reader is referred to this article for a discussion of the Munsell indexes. See pages 103-8 in the issue cited.

2. THE AMERICAN GENEALOGIST: BEING A CATALOGUE OF FAMILY HISTORIES, 5th ed. (Albany, N.Y.: Joel Munsell's Sons, 1900).

3. Marion J. Kaminkow, ed., GENEALOGIES IN THE LIBRARY OF CONGRESS: A BIBLIOGRAPHY, 3 vols. (Baltimore: Magna Carta Book Co., 1972, 1977).

4. Marion J. Kaminkow, ed., UNITED STATES LOCAL HISTORIES IN THE LIBRARY OF CONGRESS: A BIBLIOGRAPHY, 5 vols. (Baltimore: Magna Carta Book Co., 1975-77). Another good, but outdated, source for identifying county histories in the United States is Clarence Stewart Peterson, CONSOLIDATED BIBLIOGRAPHY OF COUNTY HISTORIES IN FIFTY STATES IN 1961, CONSOLIDATED 1935-1961, 2d ed. (Baltimore: Genealogical Publishing Co., 1963).

Genealogy of the HAYNES family. [Descendants of Jonathan of Haverhill, Mass., abt. 1633.] By Guy C. Haynes. New Eng. Hist. and Gen. Reg., ix (1855) 349-51.

Pedigree of the family of HAYNES of Copford Hall, co. Essex, England. By A.M. Haines of Galena, Ill. New Eng. Hist. and Gen. Reg., xxxii (1878) 310-2.

Descendants of Walter HAYNES and Peter Noyes of Sudbury, Mass. [1638]. By Frederick Haynes Newell of Washington, D.C. New Eng. Hist. and Gen. Reg. xlvii (1893) 71-5.

One line of the Haszard family. [Descendants of Thomas HAZARD of Portsmouth, R.I., 1639.] By Hon. John B. Pierce. Narragansett Hist. Reg., ii (1883-4) 45-51.

The HAZEN family. [Descendants of Edward of Rowley, Mass., before 1649.] By Henry Allen Hazen, A.M., New Haven, Conn. New Eng. Hist. and Gen. Reg., xxxiii (1879) 229-36.

Fig. 3
Example from LIST OF TITLES OF
GENEALOGICAL ARTICLES

Chapter 5

JACOBUS'S INDEXES

The genealogical indexes published by the Munsell firm probably provided the impetus for Donald Lines Jacobus, eminent genealogist, to compile indexes to American genealogical periodicals and then publish his classic INDEX TO GENEALOGICAL PERIODICALS.[1] This work was a significant attempt to index the contents of many and diverse genealogical publications in print. As Jacobus states in the introduction to volume 1 of this index:

> It covers periodicals, not family genealogies nor (with a few exceptions) occasional publications issued by historical societies in book or pamphlet form. Many historical periodicals have been consulted, but indexed only so far as strictly genealogical matter is concerned. Strictly historical matter, memoirs of persons not long dead, and other reading matter not germane to the subject of genealogy, have not been indexed.[2]

Jacobus followed the 1932 edition with a series of articles entitled "Index to Genealogical Periodicals" serialized in volumes 9 (1933) through 23 (1947) of THE AMERICAN GENEALOGIST. The information from this series of articles was later published in 1948 and 1953 as volumes 2 and 3, and carried the same title as volume 1. He did not index periodicals after 1952. Only three volumes have been published.

The foundation of Jacobus's periodical index was his own card index to THE NEW YORK GENEALOGICAL AND BIOGRAPHICAL RECORD (he initially indexed sixty-two volumes through 1931) and an index to THE NEW ENGLAND HISTORICAL AND GENEALOGICAL REGISTER (initially volumes 51-85 were indexed by Jacobus). These two serials contain a mass of genealogical data. Eventually he added other serials to his indexing project.

Fifty-one serial titles were indexed in volume 1, fifty titles in volume 2, and twenty-four titles in volume 3. Complete titles, volumes, and years of the indexed periodicals are shown in the beginning of each index in a reference list entitled "Key to Periodicals." A sample entry from this key follows:

D The Mayflower Descendant, vols. 1-28. 1899-1930.

In the entry above, "D" is the abbreviation used in the index and the reference assigned by Jacobus for this particular serial. Also shown are the title,
volume numbers included in the indexing, and the years of publication.

Jacobus also included names of eleven other titles in small type in volume 1.
Brief comments concerning each title are given. These eleven titles are listed
but not indexed.

Each of Jacobus's indexes contains a preface which adequately describes the
index, including some of its limitations. Volume 1 also has a list of fourteen
important "General Reference Sources" following the introduction.

Jacobus partially indexed a variety of genealogical periodicals and included
occasional references to historical publications containing genealogical materials.
However, he did not index periodicals which have their own general indexes,
as defined in the introductions to his indexes. For example, volumes 1-50 of
THE NEW ENGLAND HISTORICAL AND GENEALOGICAL REGISTER and those
serials published in Virginia were not indexed by Jacobus. He explained his
omission of Virginia serials in the introduction to volume 1.

> It was our hope and intention to index every genealogical publica-
> tion in the country or such portions as were not adequately covered
> by other indexes. It has been necessary to depart slightly from
> that ambition. . . . Since it was felt that our space could bet-
> ter be devoted to periodicals and sections of the country which
> need indexing much more than does Virginia and its periodicals,
> and since we did not wish our work to conflict with that of Dr.
> [Robert Armistead] Stewart and Dr. [E.G.] Swem, we reluctantly
> halted our own indexing of Virginia periodicals.[3]

The time period covered in the indexing of these three works includes periodicals published in the late 1800s through 1952. Jacobus explains the scope
and time period in the preface to volume 3:

> The first volume, published in 1932, covered the chief genealogi-
> cal periodicals through 1931, except those which provided their
> own complete general indexes. . . . The second volume, pub-
> lished in 1948, covered the fifteen years, 1932 to 1946 inclusive,
> and included a few titles (completely) which were overlooked in
> the first volume.
>
> The third volume . . . covers most of the periodicals devoted to
> genealogy or with genealogical sections for the six years, 1947 to
> 1952 inclusive.[4]

SCOPE OF THE INDEXES

Contained in these three volumes of indexes are eleven distinct sections. The
user of these indexes will therefore need to search for possible ancestral, lo-

cality, and subject references in several different divisions. The section headings in each volume follow:

Volume 1	INCLUSIVE PAGE NUMBERS
A. Name Index	no page nos.
B. Place and Subject Index	no page nos.

Volume 2	
A. Name Index	1 - 78
B. Family and Bible Records	79 -101
C. Revolutionary War Pensions	102 -115
D. Place Index	116 -148
E. Topic Index	149 -152

Volume 3	
A. Name Index	1 - 31
B. Place Index	32 - 38
C. Topic Index	39 - 40
D. "My Own Index"	41 - 72

Several examples from the Name Index and Place Index sections from volume
2, INDEX TO GENEALOGICAL PERIODICALS, are shown in Figures 4 and 5.
Surnames are alphabetical in each of the Name Index sections. Given names
are shown alphabetically along with the locality mentioned in the indexed
article, or some other identifying information may be shown. If only surnames
are given in Jacobus's indexes, these are followed by the type of record indexed, such as "Bible records" or "Family record." Jacobus's serial abbreviation is given in the entry, for example, "B4," along with the volume and
beginning page number of the article in parentheses. Many "see" references
are used.

Volume 1 indexes published locality records by the name of the city or county
and includes some separate state and country references (direct localities).
Volumes 2 and 3 use the "indirect locality approach" listing states, provinces,
and countries alphabetically and thereunder by county, city, and type of record
indexed. Jacobus briefly and adequately describes the type of record indexed.
The same periodical abbreviations are used in the place indexes as in the name
index sections. Volume number and beginning page number are also shown.

USING JACOBUS'S INDEXES

The researcher should first become familiar with INDEX TO GENEALOGICAL
PERIODICALS by taking a few minutes to scan these three volumes. One
should read the introductory sections, especially the section entitled "How to
Use This Index."

Next one should look for the name of the ancestor of interest in the Name Index, the section of personal names, from each of the three volumes. It will
be necessary to search all three name indexes individually for the ancestor of

NAME INDEX

AARONSON, JOHN; Mansfield, N. J.;
B1 (10-28; 20-73).

ABBOTT, GEORGE; (Lewis[6], Wayland,
Mass.); V1 (27-34).

ABBOTT; New Jersey families; B1 (10-
31; 12-7; 20-75).

ABEL, ANDREW; Morris Co., N. J.; B1
(10-40).

ABEL, ABELL; (Revolutionary soldiers), Md.; X2 (7-27).

ABELL, ROBERT; Preserved[2], Rehoboth,
Mass.; A1 (98-173).

ABER; Mendham, N. J.; B1 (10-41).

ABRAHAM, JAMES; Marlboro, N. J.; B1
(10-42).

ABRAHAMS, CORNELIS: Bergen, N. J.;
B1 (10-44).

ACKEN, THOMAS; Elizabethtown, N. J.;
B1 (10-45).

ACKER, PHILIP-JACOB; Lehigh Co., Pa.;
S1 (36-123).

ACKERLY, HENRY and ROBERT; English
clues; B4 (10-264).

ACKERLY, ROBERT; Brookhaven, N. Y.;
S4 (2-69); Samuel4 and Ebenezer4;
B4 (13-193).

ACKERMAN, DAVID; New York; B1 (10-
46, 49; 12-9).

ADAMS; (John-Quincy); ancestral
lines; B4 (21-167).

ADAMS; (Norfolk County, Mass.); B4
(12-258).

ADAMS; (will of Christopher, 1687),
Kittery, Me.; B4 (22-263).

ADAMS; (Eliel), Dorchester, Mass.;
S1 (35-128).

ADAMSON, JOHN; N. J.; Pa.; B1 (12-
1).

ADDAMS, RICHARD; Providence, Pa.;
S1 (37-225).

Fig. 4
Example from Jacobus's
INDEX TO GENEALOGICAL PERIODICALS, vol. 2

PLACE INDEX

ALABAMA
  Claiborne, Monroe Co.; Inscrip-
    tions; Z (77-722).
  Dallas County; Inscriptions; M
    (21-124; 23-119).
  Jefferson County; Rev. War sol-
    diers; M (24-35).
  Lawrence County; Marriage records,
    1822-26; M (27-21); marriage
    bonds, 1818-23; Z (79-609).
  Madison County; Deed Book; Z (77-
    723, 760).
  Mobile; Inscriptions of northern-
    ers; A1 (100-75).
  Morgan County; Marriage records,
    1822-47; M (23-45).
  Wilcox County; Inscriptions; Z
    (77-721).
BERMUDA
  Genealogical notes; V1 (23-176,
    259;24-50, 113, 220, 282; 25-
    44, 136, 206, 278; 26-33, 107,
    189, 295; 27-47, 144, 231, 319;
    28-33, 112, 170, 254).
  Historical; W2 (17-176, 317; 18-
    13).
  American privateering; Y1 (82-174).
CALIFORNIA
  Immigration from R. I.; S1 (26-
    232).
  Maine natives, 1850 Census; A1
    (91-276, 319).
  Passengers on the Capitol, 1849;
    A1 (91-198).
  Records of "Forty-Niners"; A1 (90-
    32).
  Voyage, San Francisco from New
    York, 1853; A1 (91-312).
  Pasadena; Inscriptions; S3 (9-1-
    15; 6-5-4).

Fig. 5
Example from Jacobus's
INDEX TO GENEALOGICAL PERIODICALS, vol. 2

interest. Look for the surname and the complete personal name. The user of these indexes will need to be aware of possible spelling variations when searching in the name indexes.

If the localities where the individual of interest and close family members were born, married, resided, and died are known, look for references to these localities in the three place indexes. It will be necessary to look under several different locality headings. The user will need to keep in mind there are three separate alphabetically arranged place name indexes--one in each volume.

Finally, look in the remaining sections for possible references to the ancestor of interest. The topic index sections include various subject headings, such as "Heraldry" and "Revolutionary War and Soldiers." The section "Family and Bible Records" may prove helpful in locating family information. This latter section should be used in conjunction with the name index sections. If the ancestor served in the revolutionary war, one should look in the section "Revolutionary War Pensions" in volume 2 and under this heading in the subject (topic) index sections.

The final section in volume 3, entitled "My Own Index," is described in the preface to volume 3. It was designed for use by Jacobus and deals chiefly with New England and New York families. A key to fifty-six sources precedes this index section. Jacobus emphasizes that entries in this section are very selective.

When looking for family names in these three indexes, one ought to check carefully for the surname of interest in each of the name index sections, since the ancestor may not be indexed separately. One should look in the index for all surnames pertaining to the pedigree, including maiden surname of the wife and mother. It may be necessary to follow several surname entries through by locating the article and determining if the names of interest are contained in the article. This will entail scanning the entire article for the ancestors of interest. The articles referenced in the name index sections are usually family genealogies. The researcher should then follow any possible leads which might be connected with the surname of interest. One can often discover hidden family genealogies by using such an approach.

Some descriptive "how to" articles and instructional material are indexed under the heading "Genealogy" in the topic index sections in volumes 1 and 3. This subject heading can be used to locate a few articles concerning research methodology published during the period Jacobus indexed periodicals.

The limitations of the three-volume INDEX TO GENEALOGICAL PERIODICALS are apparent. Like the other composite genealogical periodical indexes, they are far from comprehensive; Jacobus did not index all available genealogical periodicals published during the years available for indexing. Also, the divisions of the eleven sections may prove somewhat puzzling to the novice genealogist. It would have been helpful to have the entire three-volume index arranged or reprinted in one alphabet. Insufficient "see" references are used for referring the reader from one surname to the indexed surname. For example, the Lassell/Lasell family is indexed under "Lazell, John," without a "see" reference. Only the immigrant ancestor or most significant person in an article was indexed. Women are generally excluded from Jacobus's indexes. Names of authors are not indexed and titles of articles are generally omitted.

If used efficiently, however, Jacobus's periodical indexes will be remarkable friends. All American genealogists should be thoroughly familiar with these indexes and should use them in their research. British and Canadian genealogists may find items of interest in these works. INDEX TO GENEALOGICAL PERIODICALS is an important and useful contribution to the genealogical literature.

NOTES

1. Donald Lines Jacobus, INDEX TO GENEALOGICAL PERIODICALS, 3 vols., 1932, 1948, 1953. Reprint eds. (3 vols. in 1), Baltimore: Genealogical Publishing Co., 1963, 1973.

2. Jacobus, I:iii.

3. Jacobus, I:iv.

4. Jacobus, III:i.

Chapter 6
WALDENMAIER'S INDEXES

Following Jacobus's three volumes of periodical indexes, the next indexes to United States genealogical periodicals were edited and published by Inez Waldenmaier. Her works, published under two basic titles, partially index genealogical periodicals during the years 1956–63. Each of her two works is analyzed below.

GENEALOGICAL NEWSLETTER AND RESEARCH AIDS

GENEALOGICAL NEWSLETTER AND RESEARCH AIDS was edited and published by Inez Waldenmaier from 1955 to 1963 in Washington D.C. Volume 1 (1955) did not index genealogical periodicals, but rather was a newsletter for the American University's Institute of Genealogical Research. Volumes 2-9 were later condensed and republished as the compiler's ANNUAL INDEX TO GENEALOGICAL PERIODICALS AND FAMILY HISTORIES.

Waldenmaier's NEWSLETTER has undergone the following title changes within nine years:

> INSTITUTE NEWSLETTER, beginning with vol. 1, no.1, Spring 1955
> CLASS NEWSLETTER, 1955
> GENEALOGICAL NEWSLETTER, Spring 1956 to Spring 1960
> NEWSLETTER, Summer 1960
> GENEALOGICAL NEWSLETTER AND RESEARCH AIDS, Winter 1960
> to Summer 1963; ceased publication with vol. 9, no. 2, Summer
> 1963

Waldenmaier's NEWSLETTER partially indexes family Bible records, genealogies, titles of some periodical articles, and other miscellaneous records appearing in some of the major genealogical periodicals published in the United States for the period covered. Genealogical sources from some books are also included in her NEWS-LETTER. These indexes are published as sections in most issues of this serial under the following three general headings: (1) "Newly-Published County Histories," (2) "Index to Miscellaneous Bible Records," and (3) "Newly-Published Family Histories." Each section is described below.

51

Newly-Published County Histories

This is one of the major section headings. It indexes locality records alphabetically by state and thereunder by state general or by county as found in
periodicals and books. See Figure 6 for an example. A typical index entry
contains the following information:

state, county (followed by city, if indexed)
title of article as it appeared in the genealogical periodical, or
    other title in the publication
title of periodical (abbreviated titles are sometimes used)
date of periodical publication (page numbers are not shown)
sometimes volume numbers are included

NOTE: authors of articles are not indexed.

The following types of records are sometimes indexed under locality headings:
census records, military records, school records, vital records, wills, cemetery
records and tombstone inscriptions.

Two other similar section headings occasionally used are: "Where to
Find Newly-Published County Histories," and "County Histories." The index
entries are similar but the title of these sections varies.

Index to Miscellaneous Bible Records

This section indexes major surnames from Bible records published in genealogical
periodicals. Most of the entries refer to Bible records available at the DAR
Library in Washington, D.C. The following samples are included in this section:

surnames (listed alphabetically)
abundant "see" references from one surname to another (from one
    spouse to another)
complete name from the BR (Bible record) or FR (records that were
    kept in prayer books, account books, or family records)
date of marriage of the couple
title of periodical (or abbreviated title)
month and year of publication
page numbers are usually given where the information was located
    (these should be located by the researcher so that a search of
    children and other family members can be made)

Another similar heading used occasionally is "Bible Records from Here and
There," but the entries are like those listed above.

NEWLY PUBLISHED COUNTY HISTORIES

NEW JERSEY.
"Elder Ephraim Rittenhouse's (Primitive Baptist) record of marriages",
The National Genealogical Society Quarterly, Sept., 1961.
NEW JERSEY.
"A list of published records pertaining to history and genealogy of New
Jersey", New Jersey Genesis, Jan., 1961.
NEW JERSEY. "New Jersey people in South Carolina census of 1850", New Jersey
Genesis, July, 1961.
NEW JERSEY. "New Jersey pioneers in Texas", The Southwestern Historical
Quarterly, Jan., 1961.
NEW JERSEY.
New Jersey reader. 1961.
NEW JERSEY.
Beck, Henry C. Forgotten towns of Southern New Jersey. c1936, c1961.
NEW JERSEY. Methodist Church. The Methodist trail in New Jersey, 1836-1961.
1961.
NEW JERSEY. Pierce, Arthur D. Smugglers' Woods; jaunts and journeys in
Colonial and Revolutionary New Jersey. 1960.
NEW JERSEY. Pyne, Henry R. Ride to war; First New Jersey Cavalry. (Civil
War) 1961.
NEW JERSEY.
Stockton, Frank R. Stories of New Jersey. 1961.
NEW JERSEY, Bergen County.
List of loyalists with ancestry (nationality); gives age in 1776, occu-
pation, and land in acres, and confiscated property. 1961?

Fig. 6
Example from GENEALOGICAL NEWSLETTER
AND RESEARCH AIDS, Summer 1962.

Newly-Published Family Histories

This section indexes surnames from family histories as found in genealogical periodicals and other printed works. The following information is shown:

principal surname, listed alphabetically
title of article
title of periodical or other publication
date of publication
authors are sometimes given
"see" references from one surname to another

Another similar heading used in a few issues is "Finding List of New Family Histories and Genealogies."

ANNUAL INDEX TO GENEALOGICAL PERIODICALS AND FAMILY HISTORIES

ANNUAL INDEX TO GENEALOGICAL PERIODICALS AND FAMILY HISTORIES was edited and published by Inez Waldenmaier from 1956 to 1963 in Washington, D.C., in 8 volumes. The earlier issues of this ANNUAL INDEX are exact copies of the principal sections of Waldenmaier's NEWSLETTER (volumes 2-9) described earlier in this chapter. ANNUAL INDEX ceased publication with volume 8. The preface to the 1960 ANNUAL INDEX explains:

. . . for the past seven years the "Annual Index to Genealogical Periodicals . . ." was published, quarterly, under the title "Genealogical Newsletter . . ." and included, in addition to the annual index of current genealogical periodicals and newly-published family histories, three to six pages of queries and six pages of "filler."

In the preface to the 1962 issue, Waldenmaier mentions that it includes material found in genealogical periodicals published in 1962 and "good material" from 1961 periodicals which were overlooked in the 1961 index. She also states, "Records prior to 1860 (published in genealogical periodicals in 1962) are emphasized in this 'Annual Index. . . .'" For readers interested in Bible records, she refers the user to her GENEALOGICAL NEWSLETTER AND RESEARCH AIDS.

Waldenmaier's ANNUAL INDEX TO GENEALOGICAL PERIODICALS AND FAMILY HISTORIES contains three general sections, described below.

Surname Index

Surnames found in books and periodical articles are listed alphabetically in this section of the index. Abundant "see" references are used, referring the reader from one surname to another. For books, the author, title, place pub-

lished, and publisher are shown. For periodical articles, the title of the article, title of the serial, and date of publication are included. Sometimes the
page number is given. Like Munsell's INDEX TO AMERICAN GENEALOGIES,
only principal surnames are indexed. See Figure 7 for an example of this
index.

Place-Name Index

This section indexes locality records listed alphabetically by state and thereunder by county. This is a similar arrangement to Waldenmaier's NEWSLETTER.
The type of record indexed is shown, such as "tombstone inscriptions," along
with the title of the periodical article or book. For serials, the dates of publication and page numbers are sometimes given. For books, the year of publication is shown with the place published and name of publisher, and sometimes
the address of the publisher.

Directory

This last section contains a directory of the genealogical and historical periodicals indexed in the ANNUAL INDEX. The title of the publication is given as
well as the address where it may be obtained and its subscription cost.

CONCLUSION

Concerning Waldenmaier's ANNUAL INDEX TO GENEALOGICAL PERIODICALS
AND FAMILY HISTORIES, she reported the following information:[1] (1) approximately 100 periodicals were included in this index; (2) periodicals published
during 1956-1962/3 were indexed by Waldenmaier in this index; (3) volumes of
this index are no longer available for sale; (4) Waldenmaier did not maintain
a master cumulative index to personal names included in her ANNUAL INDEX;
(5) only major personal names from articles were included in the index; (6) a
total of 8 volumes have been published; and (7) portions of the ANNUAL IN-
DEX appeared in the GENEALOGICAL NEWSLETTER AND RESEARCH AIDS for
the inclusive years 1956-62.

It becomes apparent Waldenmaier's GENEALOGICAL NEWSLETTER has limited
use because the searcher needs to check under a variety of headings and because
the compiler did not index a significant number of sources. Her ANNUAL IN-
DEX also has limited scope and use because the indexing is not comprehensive.
As can be seen, her publications are confusing for the beginning genealogist
and appear a little disorganized. Neither of these two indexes are readily
available at genealogical libraries or repositories, but both are available at
the Genealogical Society Library in Salt Lake City.

Genealogical periodicals published during the three years following Jacobus's
INDEX TO GENEALOGICAL PERIODICALS were not indexed by Waldenmaier.

SURNAME INDEX

ABBE. "Family records of John and (1) Mary Loring Abbee, and (2) Mary Gold-
smith Abbee; allied family: Terry", McLean Co., Illinois records,
1962. DAR Library.

ACHILLES. Smith, Walter B. The Achilles family from New Hampshire, 1776-
1961. Washington, D.C.: Holmes Duplicating Co.

ACKERMAN. "David Ackerman: 380th anniversary of arrival in New Amsterdam;
related family: deVilliers." New Jersey Genesis, Oct., 1962.

ADAM. Fleming, John. Robert Adam and his circle, in Edinburgh and Rome.
1962. Harvard University Press, Cambridge 38, Massachusetts.

ADAMS. See Booker family.

ADAMS. See Griffin family.

ADAMS. See Kingsbury family.

ADAMS. See Twitchell family.

ADDIE. See Branch family.

ADE. "The Ade family and Newton County", Indiana History Bulletin, Feb.,
1962.

ADFORD. See Jaquith family.

ADKINS. "A brief history of the Adkins", (p. 15), Kansas City Genealogist,
July, 1962.

ADKINS. See Maupin family.

AKERS. See Miller family.

AKIN. See Miller-Millard family.

ALDEN. "Alden, Paybodie, Rouse, early Mayflower family", (p. 133), Bulletin
of the Seattle (Washington) Genealogical Society, Jan., 1962.

Fig. 7
Example from ANNUAL INDEX TO GENEALOGICAL
PERIODICALS AND FAMILY HISTORIES, 1962.

Robert W. Carder undertook a project of indexing genealogical periodicals for the years 1953 through 1955, but he never completed his work.[2] Therefore, a significant gap exists for the years 1953–55.

NOTES

1. Letters, Inez Waldenmaier to Kip Sperry, 14 May 1974 and 3 June 1974.

2. Letter, Robert W. Carder to Kip Sperry, 27 May 1974.

Chapter 7

GENEALOGICAL PERIODICAL ANNUAL INDEX

The most recent indexes to American, and some foreign, genealogical periodicals were initially edited by Ellen Stanley Rogers and were continued by George Ely Russell and Dr. Laird C. Towle. These important indexes are entitled GENEALOGICAL PERIODICAL ANNUAL INDEX (GPAI) and, to date, volumes 1-8 (1962-69), 13 (1974) and 14 (1975) have been published.[1] An analysis of GPAI follows:

VOLUME NUMBER	YEAR PUBLISHED	PUBLICATION YEAR OF PERIODICALS INDEXED	NUMBER OF TITLES INDEXED
[Volumes 1-4 edited by Ellen Stanley Rogers]			
1	1963	1962	78
2	1964	1963	119
3	1965	1964	116
4	1967	1965	116
[Volumes 5-8 edited by George Ely Russell]			
5	1967	1966	97
6	1969	1967	124
7	1970	1968	134
8	1973	1969	151
[Volumes 13-14 edited by Dr. Laird C. Towle]			
13	1976	1974 (few for 1973)	93
14	1977	1975	118

Since substantial differences exist in the indexing methods employed by each of the three editors of GPAI, we shall examine each set of indexes separately.[2]

GENEALOGICAL PERIODICAL ANNUAL INDEX, 1962-65

Volumes 1-4 of GPAI, edited by Ellen Stanley Rogers, index the following:

1. broad subjects (see below)
2. titles of articles
3. first key word of some titles (e.g., "Stokes Bible Record" is indexed under "Stokes")

4.   principal surname(s) in articles
5.   author (followed by a "see" reference to where the article is in-
     dexed)
6.   place names (localities)

Rogers utilizes thirteen broad subject (topical) headings which vary slightly
among issues:

    Methods
    Sources
    Military Records
    Foreign Genealogy
    Emigrants
    Heraldry (used in volumes 1, 2, and 4)
    Nomenclature
    Poems and Songs (used in volumes 1 and 2)
    Quizzes, cartoons, etc. (used in volumes 1 and 2)
    Miscellaneous
    Passenger Lists (used in volumes 3 and 4)
    Migration (used in volumes 3 and 4)
    Loyalists (used in volume 3 only)

Abundant "see" and "see also" references are used, which guide the reader
from names of authors and contributors, surnames in articles, subjects, and cer-
tain locality headings to the subject, surname, or locality under which the entry was indexed in GPAI. Records pertaining to localities are indexed using
the indirect locality approach, i.e., under the respective state and thereunder
by county. Records of foreign countries are indexed under the name of that
country or under the subject heading "Foreign Genealogy."

Books reviewed are listed together alphabetically in a separate section by author
or title for each included year. Volume 2 (1963) lists thirteen newspaper references under the title "Newspaper Key." Volume 3 (1964) lists twenty-two
newspaper references under the heading "Newspaper Key--Columns which Contain Genealogy." Volume 3 also has a list of thirty-seven "Family Periodicals."

A typical entry (see Figure 8) from the first four volumes of GPAI includes the
following:

    surname or subject
    title (underlined) of the article as printed in the periodical
    author's name (in parentheses)
    abbreviation of the title of. the periodical (as found in "Key to
        Genealogical Periodicals")
    volume and issue numbers
    inclusive pages from the article indexed

Related surnames in the article are also shown in parentheses in the index entry. These surnames are preceded by a plus (+) sign in the index. Each of
the four volumes contains an addenda.

O'Neale. William & Rhoda (Lanning)
O'Neale of Trenton, N. J., & Wash-
ington, D. C.; Their Ancestry
& Descendants (by Lewis D. Cook)
NGS 53-2, p 83-90
Opdycke & LaTourrette of Hunterdon
Co., N. J. (by Lewis D. Cook)
NGS 53-4, p 271-5
Oregon Notes ORE 4-3, p 150
Ore., research. Excerpts. from the
Portland Oregonian, 16 Oct. 1938
(+Applegate) (by R. J. Hendricks)
ORE 3-7, p 125; 3-8, p 130; 4-4
p 153-5
Ore., research. Oregon Research (by
Howard G. Humphrey) ORE 4-1, p 140
Ore., Clackamas Co. Marriage Records
MHT 6-3, p 13-20; 6-4, p 25-7;
7-1, p 13-18; 7-2, p 29-34
Ore., Clackamas Co. Early Days in
Estacada (by E. L. Meyers) MHT
7-2, p 24-5
Ore., Clackamas Co. Bonney Cemetery
(+Bonney) (by Georgie Tolleson)
MHT 7-2, p 26
Ore., Clackamas Co. Viola Cemetery
MHT 6-3, p 11-12
Ore., Clackamas Co. History of Upper
Logan School Dist., No. 8 (by Pearl
Kirchem) MHT 6-3, p 5-10
Ore., Clackamas Co. Clarks Cemetery
(also Johnson, Boyer cemeteries -
1 marker) (by Georgie Tolleson)
MHT 7-1, p 7
Ore., Columbiana Co. Names from
Elzie George General Store Ledger,
1887-1892 (by Mrs. Elmer V. Ander-
son) POR 15-2, p 25

Fig. 8
Example from GENEALOGICAL PERIODICAL ANNUAL
INDEX, vol. 4, 1965. Used by permission

Rogers offers the following explanation in the preface to the index to volume 1 (1962):

> Authors are also included in the INDEX, the term author designat-
> ing the person who wrote, contributed, compiled or collected the
> material. A modified system of cross reference has been adapted
> to make the GPA INDEX especially helpful to researchers. Cor-
> rections appearing in a later issue are keyed to the original article.
> Where a title is not given or is not sufficiently explanatory, I have
> provided a title or added an information note. In all cases, the
> primary objective has been to provide the researcher with a con-
> cise, convenient guide.[3]

A section entitled "Key to Genealogical Periodicals" is included and it contains the following explanations for each periodical indexed:

> abbreviation used in the indexing
> title of periodical
> name and address of publisher
> editor's name
> frequency of publication
> which volume was indexed
> subscription cost
> pages per issue
> size of pages
> special features
> other similar information

GENEALOGICAL PERIODICAL ANNUAL INDEX, 1966-69

George Ely Russell used a more comprehensive indexing approach in volumes
5-8 of GPAI than that employed by Rogers. The indexing methodology used by
Russell is concisely defined in the introduction to volume 5 of GPAI:

> Subject only to limitations of space, GPAI makes every effort to
> provide sufficient cross-references and identifying information to
> enable the searcher to judge whether or not a particular item merits
> examination. Records pertaining to individuals are indexed with
> full name, year of birth (or marriage), name of wife, states of
> residence, and type of record (e.g., family record, pension claim,
> service record, genealogy of descendants). Source records are in-
> dexed by state or province, county, town, village, type of record,
> and inclusive names and dates. Methodological materials are in-
> dexed under the general heading "Methodology" as well as the
> specific technical subject (e.g., microfilm, gravestone transcribing,
> maps). Authors of major genealogies, essays, or other original
> contributions are indexed by full name with the short titles of their
> works. Names of abstractors, transcribers, copiests, and contribu-
> tors of undocumented short family accounts are not indexed. Criti-
> cal book reviews are indexed by subject.[4]

As explained by the compiler, GPAI 1966-69 does not index queries, brief news notes, newspaper columns, family magazines, society news, book notices, or other items "of limited significance." Some material from historical periodicals has been indexed, however. Surname magazines are indexed under the major surname of the periodical.

In volumes 5-8 of GPAI, the earliest or principal male name appearing in an article is indexed. Sometimes the name of the principal son is also included. The year of birth, marriage, or death is sometimes given along with personal names. The name of the ancestor's wife is not indexed separately but her name is included with her husband's name in the index entry for him. Accounts of the families of married daughters are indexed under the husband's name. Records pertaining to localities are indexed by state and thereunder by county and town (the indirect locality approach). Book reviews are indexed by subject, personal name or locality, and some are indexed separately by title. See Figure 9 for an example from GPAI 1969.

GPAI 1966-69 partially indexes all major genealogical periodicals published in the United States as well as the following five foreign serials:

IRISH ANCESTOR
IRISH GENEALOGIST
ONTARIO GENEALOGICAL SOCIETY BULLETIN
SCOTTISH GENEALOGIST
THE GENEALOGISTS' MAGAZINE (London)

Each issue of GPAI 1966-69 contains a section entitled "Periodicals Indexed" which shows the following information:

abbreviation used in the indexing
title of periodical
name and address of publisher
usually the subscription cost

The following explanation of how items are indexed in GPAI 1966-69 is offered by Russell:

Regarding indexing in GPAI, entries are prepared only when a significant amount of genealogical or biographical data is given about an individual. For example: a published abstract of a pension claim file would be indexed under the name of the soldier (full name). Appearance of a name on a list of tax payers would not result in an index entry. If a published genealogy follows the married daughters' families, an entry would be prepared for each husband if the couple's children are provided in the account. In a published genealogy following only the families of sons (with the same surname), GPAI would have an entry only for the progenitor, describing as 'gen of desc.'[5]

MASSACHUSETTS, Barnstable Co., Eastham marr recs
    1795-1844   NER 123:2:117 123:3:198
    Harwich & Chatham vital recs, by Vernon R.
      Jickerson (c1969) book review   CDS 6:6:5
    Berkshire Co., Hancock vital recs, 1767-1832
                      SCS 6:2:58 6:3:108
    N. Adams, names in King autograph album,
      1847, 1850   DSGR 32:4:156
    Hampden Co., Springfield, Judge Pynchon's marr
      recs, 1685-1711   NER 123:4:258
    Hampshire Co., Hadley, births & deaths, 1794-
      1816 [Phelps private record]   NER 123:1:16
    Nantucket, hist & gens, by Alexander Starbuck
      (1969) book review   G&H 2:1:59
    Plymouth Co. marr recs, 1692-1746 (repr 1968)
      book review   NYR 100:1:52
    N. Abington, names in autograph book, 1875-
      1881   SCS 6:1:28
    Suffolk Co., Boston "Pilot" [Catholic] newspa-
      per notices [Irishmen], 1830-1833
                      IreG 3:12:520
    Boston Tea Party members, 1773
                   DAR 103:10:829
    Dorchester, death recs, 1800   GP 5:12:18
MASSACHUSETTS Centinel, marr notices, 1785-94,
    by Chas. K. Bolton (1900, repr 1965) bk rev
                      TRI 9:1:3
    gen sources, research outline   SWG 7:1:1
    marr recs prior to 1800, by Frederick W. Bail-
      ey (1914, repr 1968) bk rev   NGSQ 57:3:230
                  NYR 100:1:52 GH 23:2:66
    pilgrim fathers, English ancestry & homes, by
      Chas. E. Banks (1929, repr c1969) bk review
                      GH 23:4:386
    Winthrop fleet of 1630, by Chas E. Banks
      (1930, repr c1968) book review   GH 23:3:297
MASSER, Henry (m1802) w Barbara Baldy, fam rec
                      CP 3/69:16
MASSEY, Drury (b1775 S.C.) w Lowry & Vashti Gor-
    han, Tenn., Ala., family   DSGQ 7:1:39

Fig. 9
Example from GENEALOGICAL PERIODICAL
ANNUAL INDEX, 1969

Russell has stated, "The goal of GPAI is to include all English-language genealogical periodicals. No periodical is deliberately excluded."[6] GPAI by no
means indexes all English-language genealogical periodicals as stated. However,
GPAI does index the most significant genealogical periodicals published in the
United States, and it is the most sophisticated index of its kind in genealogy.
One reason that GPAI does not index more serials is that "GPAI does not subscribe to periodicals. The standard arrangement is for publishers to contribute
their periodicals to GPAI for indexing and inclusion."[7] This is a limitation
in the coverage of this index since the compiler did not actively purchase
serials for inclusion in the index.

A number of periodicals published during Rogers's editorship, but unavailable to
her, were indexed by Russell in his issues of GPAI. It is essential, therefore,
that all issues of GPAI be checked to obtain genealogical references in periodicals published. GPAI is particularly useful in locating family genealogies, especially if the surname is uncommon, as well as identifying published locality
records.

Russell is presently indexing genealogical periodicals which were published during the years 1970-73.[8] He has discontinued indexing periodicals published
after 1 January 1974.

GENEALOGICAL PERIODICAL ANNUAL INDEX: KEY TO THE GENEALOGICAL LITERATURE

Volume 13 of GPAI, edited by Laird C. Towle, is one of the latest in this
series of indexes to some English-language genealogical periodicals. In volume
13, 1974, Towle indexes personal names (surnames and given names), published
locality records, and many 1974 book reviews. Personal names are followed
by helpful identifying information, such as year of birth, name of wife, etc.
The name of the wife is not cross-indexed, however. A few subject (topical)
headings have also been used, for example "American Indian Genealogy,"
"Heraldry," "Methodology," "Royal and Noble Genealogy," and others. The
user will need to scan the index to determine what subject headings have been
used by the compiler. Items indexed are in capital letters making the index
easy to use. Names of authors of articles, compilers, and titles of articles
are not indexed. The format is similar to, but not identical to, volumes 5-8
of GPAI.

The introduction to GPAI 1974 is followed by a listing of abbreviations used in
the work and a list of ninety-three serial titles which have been indexed. This
is about 50 percent of American and British genealogical periodicals available
in 1974, not counting family and surname magazines, genealogical newsletters,
and bulletins. Family and surname periodicals are indexed by the major surname
only and these titles are not listed separately.

A significant number of genealogical periodicals published in the United States,
Canada, and Great Britain are not indexed in GPAI 1974. The introduction to

volume 13 states that all periodicals indexed were donated to the compiler for
that purpose. Apparently no attempt was made to increase the scope of this
index by locating additional periodicals in libraries or by subscribing to genealogical periodicals. It is important to be aware of such limitations when using
this index. Some of the better known serial titles which have been excluded
from the GPAI 1974 (volume 13) index are the following:

CONNECTICUT ANCESTRY
THE CONNECTICUT NUTMEGGER
DEEP SOUTH GENEALOGICAL QUARTERLY
FAMILY HISTORY
GENEALOGICAL JOURNAL
THE GENEALOGICAL MAGAZINE OF NEW JERSEY
GENEALOGISTS' MAGAZINE
GENEALOGY DIGEST
THE GEORGIA GENEALOGICAL MAGAZINE
THE IDAHO GENEALOGICAL SOCIETY QUARTERLY
ILLIANA GENEALOGIST
THE KANSAS CITY GENEALOGIST
THE MARYLAND AND DELAWARE GENEALOGIST
MEMOIRES
NEW ORLEANS GENESIS
THE NEW YORK GENEALOGICAL AND BIOGRAPHICAL RECORD
ST. LOUIS GENEALOGICAL SOCIETY QUARTERLY
THE SOUTHERN GENEALOGIST'S EXCHANGE QUARTERLY
STIRPES

GENEALOGICAL PERIODICAL ANNUAL INDEX: KEY TO THE GENEALOGICAL LITERATURE, 1975

This sixty-two-page composite periodical index, also edited by Laird C. Towle,
is more comprehensive than GPAI 1974. One hundred eighteen periodical
titles are indexed, twenty-five more than in GPAI 1974. Included are some
of the important titles which were omitted in GPAI 1974. Corrections to GPAI
1974 are also included in the introduction to this index. Some periodicals
published in 1974 are indexed in GPAI 1975. Refer to Figure 10 for an example from GPAI 1975.

The index headings are similar to those in the earlier GPAI series, although
the subject heading "Methodology" is expanded to include more entries. Titles
of thirty-nine family magazines are indexed under the major surname of that
serial title. Many book reviews are indexed in GPAI 1975.

CONCLUSION

The genealogist should first become familiar with the scope and limitations of
each of the three sets of GPAI. The user of these indexes would do best to

BRUNN, Rev Friedrich b1819, Ger, biog note,
sermon & letters CHI 48:4:116
BRYANT, William Cullen, index to geneal, bk
rev CDS 12:X:22
BUCK, Frederick bc1771 w Eliza Reily & Harriet
Mahony, Co Cork, Ir, biog & geneal IA
7:1:15
John b1793 w Eliza Cook, VA, KY, OH, IL,
fam rec GT 11:1:16
BUCKNER, William m1773 w Elizabeth Smith,
Bible rec VA 13:3:70
BUETTNER, George L bc1875, MO, recoll of
printing career CHI 47:2:62
BULL, John bc1794, Ir, KY, natural rec KA
11:2:80
BULLER, Thomas b1808 w Emily Brignac & Eve-
lina Carentin, LA, fam letters 1856-
1863 & notes LGR 21:2:157
BULLOCK, Samuel m1675 w Thankful, MA, ident-
ity of wife PCH 3:36
BUNCH, fams of NC, KY, MO, bk rev GH 29:2:240
BURBANK, Daniel Jr. b1770 w Margaret Pynchon,
MA, IL, fam rec GT 11:1:9
BURGESS, fams in US, bk rev GH 29:1:56
BURK, Lemmon m1828 w Rachel Green, MD, IA,
Bible rec HH 9:3:117
BURKS, John W b1826 w Louisa N Tucker, AL, TN,
Bible rec & fam rec AN 22:3:132
BURLINGHAM, Eliphalet bc1785, OH, geneal, bk
rev GH 29:2:239
BURNHAM, Thomas b1722 w Judith, Bible rec RRS
4:2:98
BURNEY, David b1756, NC, GA, MS, Rev War pen-
sion abstr GGM 52/53:167
BURR, Timothy b1785 w Rachel Hart Thrift, MA,
LA, fam rec LGR 22:2:168
BURRIS, James Salter, ances, bk rev AN 22:3:
111
BURROUGHES, Jacob f1742 w Mary, VA, will VA
13:2:47
surname period, see BERRY

Fig. 10
Example from GENEALOGICAL PERIODICAL
ANNUAL INDEX, 1975

begin searching first in the most current volumes, working backwards to volume one. The reason for this approach is that the more current issues are more comprehensive and often include data overlooked in the earlier volumes.

When looking for an ancestral name, one should look for any possible references to that surname for the localities of interest. Also look for possible spelling variations. If an entry is found, the index reference will give the title of the serial in abbreviated format along with the volume number, issue number, and beginning page number. Determine the full title of the serial from the front introductory section. When seeking published locality records, first look for the state of interest but also check under the region and country. The subject and topical headings used in GPAI are not consistent in all issues. Therefore, the researcher must peruse each issue to find these. The genealogist wishing to know of published material on a particular subject should look under the heading "Methodology." One should not overlook other possible subject headings.

None of the issues of GPAI has comprehensive name indexes. Mostly principal names in an article are indexed--such as the most significant individual mentioned, or the immigrant ancestor. Brief ancestral sketches are generally excluded from indexing, as are other published materials.

Genealogists should be aware of these indexes--their scope and limitations. United States and Canadian libraries serving genealogists should have GPAI in their collections and should maintain a standing order for them because they are the current periodical indexes. GPAI is useful to genealogists and librarians in locating personal names in genealogical periodicals as well as published locality records and book reviews.

NOTES

1. Volumes 1-4 were published by Genealogical Recorders, Bladensburg, Maryland. Volumes 5-8 were compiled and published by George Ely Russell (Lombardy Drive, Woodmere South, Route 3, Box 157, Middletown, Maryland 21769). Volumes 13 and 14 were compiled and published by Dr. Laird C. Towle (Yankee Bookman, 3602 Maureen Lane, Bowie, Maryland 20715). Some of the earlier volumes of GPAI are now out of print.

2. GPAI has been briefly discussed in the GENEALOGICAL JOURNAL 1 (1972): 20; and THE COLONIAL GENEALOGIST 8 (1976): 68. See also the article by Kip Sperry and Roger Scanland, "Searching the Genealogical Literature: Periodical Indexes," NATIONAL GENEALOGICAL SOCIETY QUARTERLY 63 (1975): 186-93; and Laird C. Towle, GENEALOGICAL PERIODICALS: A NEGLECTED TREASURE (Bowie, Md.: Yankee Bookman, 1977).

3. Ellen Stanley Rogers, preface to GENEALOGICAL PERIODICAL ANNUAL INDEX 1 (1962).

4. GENEALOGICAL PERIODICAL ANNUAL INDEX 5 (1966): iii.

5. Letter, George Ely Russell to Kip Sperry, 30 April 1974.

6. GENEALOGICAL PERIODICAL ANNUAL INDEX 8 (1969): ii.

7. Ibid.

8. Letters, George Ely Russell to Kip Sperry, 14 February 1974 and 20 September 1974. Mr. Russell is working on a cumulative periodical index for the years 1966-73.

Chapter 8

TOPICAL INDEX OF GENEALOGICAL QUARTERLIES

A set of current indexes to some genealogical periodicals published in the United States began in 1973 and is entitled TOPICAL INDEX OF GENEALOGICAL QUARTERLIES. The 1973, 1974, and 1975 indexes were compiled by Geraldine Bailey. Isabelle Rolland cocompiled the 1973 index. They have been published by the St. Louis Genealogical Society and are intended to be published annually.[1]

Over one hundred titles of genealogical periodicals, and a few family magazines, are shown in the first section of these indexes, entitled "St. Louis Genealogical Society Periodical Exchange List." The 1973 list has 116 titles; there are 122 titles in the 1974 list, and 128 in the 1975 list. Only titles published in the United States are included. One periodical, the ACADIAN GENEALOGY EXCHANGE, published in Covington, Kentucky, will be of interest to Canadian genealogists. Two query indexes, LINKAGE FOR ANCESTRAL RESEARCH and QUERY NAME INDEX, are shown in the "Periodicals Exchange List" for 1973; QUERY NAME INDEX is shown in the 1974 and 1975 indexes.

The serial titles in the Exchange List are not alphabetical by title but are arranged chronologically according to a numeric code assigned each title, such as 01.1 or 51.1. The arrangement is alphabetical by state. The complete address from which the serial can be obtained is shown, as well as the specific issues indexed in that issue of the TOPICAL INDEX.

Only those periodicals exchanged with the St. Louis Genealogical Society are indexed. Noticeably absent from this list of serials are titles of the major genealogical periodicals published in the United States, such as THE AMERICAN GENEALOGIST, THE DETROIT SOCIETY FOR GENEALOGICAL RESEARCH MAGAZINE, THE GENEALOGICAL HELPER, GENEALOGICAL JOURNAL, NATIONAL GENEALOGICAL SOCIETY QUARTERLY, THE NEW ENGLAND HISTORICAL AND GENEALOGICAL REGISTER, THE NEW YORK GENEALOGICAL AND BIOGRAPHICAL RECORD, THE PENNSYLVANIA GENEALOGICAL MAGAZINE, and THE VIRGINIA GENEALOGIST, to name a few. Apparently serials not exchanged with the ST. LOUIS GENEALOGICAL SOCIETY QUARTERLY are not included in their index. This is a serious limitation of the TOPICAL INDEX and researchers should be aware of this deficiency.

Following the listing of serials included in the index, the work is divided into two general sections, analyzed separately below.

TOPICS

Part one indexes topics from periodical articles. These are listed under locality headings for the United States. States are alphabetically arranged and then alphabetical by counties. A "General Information" section is under some state headings.

Under the localities, topical headings are listed along with a numeric code used to identify the title of the serial. Also shown are the issue number and page number where the reference can be located in the periodical. The reader will then need to find the particular code in the list of exchange periodicals at the front of the index in order to determine the title of that serial. Figure 11 shows entries from the Topics section.

Canada and a few other foreign countries follow the listing for the United States. The arrangement under each foreign country is similar to that for the United States. These listings of countries are followed by other index sections:

1973 TOPICAL INDEX	1974 TOPICAL INDEX
Maps	Research Sources and Aids:
Military	Church Records
Religion	Immigration and Migration
Research Sources and Aids	Records*
Foreign Sources	Land and Court Records
General Information	Military and Pension Records*
Index of Quarterlies	Research Sources (General)*
Surname Index of Quarterlies	Special Aids and Suggestions*
Miscellaneous	Writing and Publishing Manuscripts
	General Information*

* headings used in the 1975 TOPICAL INDEX

General research topics are indexed under the headings "Research Sources and Aids," "Special Aids and Suggestions," and "General Information." Full titles or partial titles of articles are shown under each heading. These sections contain useful references to articles concerning research methodology, paleography, indexing, patriotic societies, articles on surnames, genealogical correspondence, calendar changes, heraldry, publishing, and others. Unfortunately, some of the most scholarly articles on these and related subjects are not included in the TOPICAL INDEX since they are contained in various periodicals not covered by this index.

SURNAMES

Part two of the TOPICAL INDEX is an alphabetical list of surnames followed

MAINE

YORK COUNTY
An Old Cemetery (City of York, Maine)   12.2   b   4

MARYLAND

BALTIMORE COUNTY
Birth Records (First & St. Stephens United
   Church of Christ) (Death Records)*   20.2   a   5
Baptismal & Birth Records (St. Peter the
   Apostle Roman Catholic Church)*   20.2   a   30
Muster Rolls (Maryland Militia, War 1812) 20.2   c 115

CAROLINE COUNTY
Marriages (United Methodist) 1878-82   22.5   d 124

DORCHESTER COUNTY
1800 Census*   20.2   b   99

FREDERICK COUNTY
Servicemen in the American Revolution   20.2   d 167

HOWARD COUNTY
Cemetery (Western Howard County)   20.2   b   69

PRINCE GEORGES COUNTY
Forest Memorial Church Cemetery   20.3   g   20
Immanuel Meth. Episc. Church South Cem.* 20.3   a   3
St. Paul's Episcopal Chruch Cemetery*   20.3   i   39
Across the Years in Prince Georges Co.   20.3   d   46

QUEEN ANNES COUNTY
St. John's Parish Register Book (Birth,etc) 20.2   b   73

SOMERSET COUNTY
1800 Census*   20.2   a   24

Fig. 11
Example from TOPICAL INDEX OF 1975 GENEALOGICAL
QUARTERLIES, p. 11, "Topics" section

by one, and occasionally two, of the following abbreviations, which indicate the type of record where that surname appears.

AC - Ancestor Chart
B - Bible Record
BI - Biography
CM - Cemetery, Grave Markers
CT - Court Records (other than Probate Records)
D - Deeds and Land Records
F - Family Records and Family History
L - Letters and Diaries, Account Books
M - Military Service, Pensions, Bounties
MS - Miscellaneous
O - Obituaries
TX - Taxes (Real Estate and Personal)
W - Wills, Estates, Administrations
* - Continued Records
** - Bride's Surname (Oldest Marriage in Family Record)

Next is the numeric code used to refer the reader to the serial indexed, refer-ence to the issue indexed, and the page number of the article where that sur-name appears. If a surname of interest is located in this index, the researcher will want to read the pages before and after that page mentioned, since ad-ditional references to the surname may be available in that particular periodical.

Approximately 1,500 surnames are contained in this final section of each annual TOPICAL INDEX. Only major surnames from articles are indexed, however. This section is a good locating tool for the more uncommon family surnames. See Figure 12 for an example from the surname section.

An example entry from the surname portion of this index follows:

ADAMS - B 15.1 d 178

Explanation of this entry:

ADAMS - surname indexed in the TOPICAL INDEX
B - Bible record
15.1 - title of periodical indexed, in this case, HAWKEYE HERI-
TAGE, published by the Iowa Genealogical Society
d - issue indexed, in this case, Volume 10, number 4, October 1975
178 - page 178 for that reference

CONCLUSION

The overall format of the TOPICAL INDEX gives one the impression of com-pactness and incompleteness. The print is small and sometimes faint, making portions of the index difficult to read. The printing of the 1975 index is better than the two earlier issues. Each issue is stapled between paper covers.

CALDWELL—BI	25.1	a	5
CALDWELL—F	43.7	d	139
CALFEE—F	16.3	c	73
CALLAWAY—F	43.11	c	45
CAMPBELL—F	13.1	b	147
CAMPBELL—F	13.18	c	209
CAMPBELL—F	25.5	a	--
CAMPBELL—F	43.1	b	63
CAMPBELL—AC	47.2	a	9
CAMRON—B	13.19	b	3
CANNON—F	13.6	b	13
CANTRELL—B**	42.4	b	93
CAPWELL—AC	47.6	b	103
CARNAHAN—BI	04.2	b	13
CARNELL—CM	42.4	b	91
CARNEY—AC	05.5	d	164
CARNHAN—F	37.1	c	71
CARPENTER—F	13.9	b	35
CARPENTER—F	19.2	--	--
CARR—B	16.2	b	23
CARRELL—O	13.8	a	11
CARRICK—B**	25.5	c	--
CARROLL—AC	06.2	d	198
CARSON—AC	05.5	d	162
CARSON—F	13.9	b	--
CARTER—B	04.2	d	10
CARTER—AC	06.2	b	53
CARTER—F	13.9	a	38
CARTER—B**	18.1	d	188
CARTER—B**	47.8	a	65

Fig. 12
Example from the surname section of
TOPICAL INDEX OF 1975 GENEALOGICAL QUARTERLIES

Although it has a table of contents, it lacks a preface, introduction, examples, or other explanations of how to use the index. An exception is a brief explanation given in the 1975 index. The 1973 TOPICAL INDEX contains nineteen pages, the 1974 index has twenty-one pages, and the 1975 index has twenty-six pages. This index is an attempt to index United States genealogical serials succinctly. Genealogical queries are not indexed; neither are authors of articles nor book reviews indexed.

In spite of these limitations, it is a welcome tool which may prove helpful to the genealogist attempting to identify locality records in print, articles concerning basic research techniques, and as a source for locating surnames in some of the periodical literature published in the United States for the years indexed. The indexes are economically priced. The St. Louis indexes will not, however, entirely replace GENEALOGICAL PERIODICAL ANNUAL INDEX. The researcher should use each volume of the TOPICAL INDEX in conjunction with GENEALOGICAL PERIODICAL ANNUAL INDEX.

NOTES

1. St. Louis Genealogical Society, TOPICAL INDEX OF GENEALOGICAL QUARTERLIES, comp. by Geraldine Bailey (St. Louis: St. Louis Genealogical Society, 1973--). Address: 1617 South Brentwood Blvd., Suite 261, St. Louis, Missouri 63144.

Chapter 9

QUERY INDEXES

Many genealogical periodicals and a few newspapers have query sections designed to help genealogists in their research. A query is a method whereby an individual submits a genealogical inquiry pertaining to a particular personal name, family, or genealogical problem, with the intention of contacting others doing research on the same name or pedigree problem. A query is a method of requesting, and also sharing, genealogical information. Other researchers may be working on the same line and these researchers can sometimes be found by checking queries. If located, genealogists may then be able to pool research efforts as well as share pedigree information.

There are three general classifications of queries: (1) the surname query, (2) the surname and state query, and (3) the specific problem query. In the surname query, the surname or surnames of interest are given along with the name and address of the person submitting the inquiry. The surname and state query is similar except that the states where the family resided are also shown. The specific problem query lists the details of the research problem, such as names, date and place of birth, marriage and death, and names of close family members. Each type of query has its advantages and limitations; however, the specific problem query is probably the most useful since more information is given which might help others in their research, and it will help in identifying the pedigree problem.[1]

Like other genealogical sources, genealogical queries have their limitations. George E. McCracken has stated in a book review of one of the query indexes, "We are somewhat skeptical of the value of queries, since there is danger that if they are relied on, it may become a case of the blind leading the blind, but one may discover another who is interested in the same line and some value may be derived from correspondence."[2] Even in this critical evaluation of queries, McCracken sees some value in the usefulness of queries in genealogical research.

Genealogical queries have their rightful place in genealogical research, especially in the preliminary survey. Queries are a tool very often used by the amateur--but some professionals use queries as well.

Some publications which print queries will do so at no cost while others charge a small fee for this service. A genealogist may benefit from submitting genealogical queries, particularly on a difficult pedigree puzzle. By getting the pedigree problem in print, the researcher may be able to contact someone else working on or interested in that same family.

Some periodicals publish replies to queries. Examples are the FRENCH CANADIAN AND ACADIAN GENEALOGICAL REVIEW and THE MARYLAND GENEALOGICAL SOCIETY BULLETIN. This is a useful service, especially when these queries are indexed and the genealogist has easy access to them.

ACCESS TO QUERIES

Indexes to genealogical queries are helpful to the researcher in two ways: (1) they refer the searcher to a published inquiry where more information on the ancestor may be available, and (2) the query refers the searcher to the name and address of the person who submitted the inquiry for publication.

Some genealogical periodicals and newspapers which publish queries index their own queries in each issue or through separately published query indexes. These indexes will provide the researcher access to vast amounts of genealogical data. Genealogical queries are not indexed in GENEALOGICAL PERIODICAL ANNUAL INDEX, or in the other composite periodical indexes described earlier in this book.

THE GENEALOGICAL HELPER is one example of a periodical which publishes its query indexes in each issue in which the queries appear. The TRI-STATE TRADER, a weekly newspaper published in Knightstown, Indiana, has a genealogy section which publishes queries; it indexes queries in each weekly issue of the newspaper under the headings "Query Surname Index," "Query Index by County," and "Other States." The TRI-STATE TRADER also publishes separate annual query indexes, entitled TRI-STATE TRADER GENEALOGICAL QUERIES.

There are three significant composite indexes to genealogical queries contained in American periodicals. Each of these indexes is described separately below, followed by a section outlining several miscellaneous indexes to genealogical queries.

GENEALOGIST'S WEEKLY QUERY INDEX

GENEALOGIST'S WEEKLY QUERY INDEX was published by the Genealogist's Weekly Query Exchange from 1957 to 1963. The place of publication varied among Lansing, Iowa; Vinton, Iowa; Greeley, Iowa; and Casey, Illinois. An extract from the index appears in Figure 13.

Highsmith, Sarah (Allison); Ill., Ore. ca. 1890;
  Genealogical Forum of Portland, Oregon 10:60 Ap '61 455
Hightower, Sally; m. Walker; N. C. , Tenn. 1813;
  "Ansearchin'" News 8:30 Ja '61 19
Hill Family;
  Ft. Worth Genealogical Society Bulletin 4:9 Je '61
Hillis Family; Tenn.
  Ft. Worth Genealogical Society Bulletin 4L9 Je '61
Holmes, Joseph W.; Ohio, Ill.
  Ancestral Notes 8 My '61 E-340
Holmes, Mary (_____); Ohio, Ill.
  Ancestral Notes 8 My '61 E-340
Holmes, Mary Missouri; b. 1829; Ohio, Ill.
  Ancestral Notes 8 My '61 E-340
Holmes, Paulina Jane; b. 1816; m. 1838, Kirkham; Ohio, Ill.
  Ancestral Notes 8 My '61 E-340
Holmes, Phoebe; m. 1827, Taylor;
  Gene-A-Card 373
Horne, Abashai; b. ca. 1743;
  Southern Genealogist's Exchange 3:22 Spring '61 314
Horne, Abisha; b. ca. 1743;
  Southern Genealogist's Exchange 3:22 Spring '61 314

Fig. 13
Example from GENEALOGIST'S WEEKLY QUERY INDEX

GENEALOGIST'S WEEKLY QUERY INDEX is a personal name index to approximately twenty genealogical periodicals and to the genealogical pages of two weekly newspapers. Included are name indexes to query sections in genealogical periodicals and to the HARTFORD TIMES genealogical page. This query index discontinued publication in 1963.

The following information is given in this index (if included in the query): full personal name or surname, maiden name, surname of husband, date of birth, marriage or death, if immigrant or if military service, state of residence, title of publication where the query appeared, volume number, publication date, and page number. A query number is sometimes shown. Entries are alphabetically arranged by surname. The alphabetical arrangement is continued with each issue. Therefore, each issue is not alphabetical from A through Z. This index is available at relatively few genealogical libraries. Its value is limited because it is out of date.

LINKAGE FOR ANCESTRAL RESEARCH

LINKAGE FOR ANCESTRAL RESEARCH (LFAR) has been edited and published by Mrs. Frank N. (Mary Tune) Reeder from March 1967 to the present. Place of publication is Albuquerque, New Mexico.

LFAR indexes only surnames, as found in genealogical queries. It was intended to be a quarterly but it is published irregularly. Only queries in periodicals published in the United States are indexed by Reeder; however, each issue has a separate section for queries that indicate a foreign location. Reeder states, "Each issue is complete within itself."[3]

Surnames are listed alphabetically followed by one or more code numbers, which refer the reader to the periodical where the query is published. The month of publication is given along with the specific query number. An example of LFAR can be seen in Figure 14. This index is difficult to use for common surnames because of the multiple references, but may prove useful in locating uncommon surnames.

There is a separate listing of periodicals indexed, which also shows the address, frequency of publication, and cost of each periodical.

QUERY NAME INDEX

QUERY NAME INDEX (QNI), compiled by Roy and Barie Colbert, was published from April 1973 to January 1975 by the Homestead Press in Kenmore, Washington.

Alms 79Su760
Alpin 61Oct419
Alsop 87Dec25
Alspach 8Oct18
Alsup 87Dec25
Altic 27Nov23
Alumbaugh 79Su676
Ames 79W606/79W786/87Dec28
Amiss 79Sp574
Amsden 45Spt7
Amrine 75Dec6
Andersen 61Oct392
Anderson 2Nov I96/10Oct609/26Spt8/26
       Sept19/27Nov6/32F76/35Nov22/35
       Nov23/41Spt11/34-260-2/34-261-2/
       61Oct392/69-211-6/82Jun69
Andes 69-212-15

Fig. 14
Example from LINKAGE FOR ANCESTRAL RESEARCH,
vol. 6, January 1973

Query Indexes

The most comprehensive of the query indexes, QNI indexes surnames and complete personal names from queries as published in over one hundred United States and Canadian genealogical and family periodicals. QNI discontinued publication with their January 1975 issue.

Entries are alphabetical by surname and show the full name as listed in the query, the state or states (or foreign country) where the person was known to have lived, and the code number of the periodical from which the entry was taken. Given names are grouped together after the surname. Married women are indexed under both their maiden surname and married surname. For an example of QNI, see Figure 15.

Each issue contains a reference section where the periodicals are listed numerically by code number. In this section the following items are shown: titles, publisher's address, frequency of publication and cost of the periodical, and volume and issue number of the periodical that published the original query. Each issue also contains an addendum of names omitted in the initial indexing.

The researcher is given sufficient information to locate the original query in a genealogical periodical; or, if the periodical is unavailable, the researcher can write to Homestead Press, since they offer a photocopy service to subscribers. According to the introduction to each issue of QNI, Homestead Press will mail a photocopy of the original query for a nominal fee (more is charged for non-subscribers).

The following uses of QUERY NAME INDEX are outlined in the introduction to the January 1974 issue:

> This index can be a most valuable aid to you in your research,
> 1) as an aid in contacting others that are researching like names,
> 2) provide your own query needs for greater exposure when published
> by a participating organization shown in the REFERENCE SECTION,
> because of QNI's nation-wide circulation, and 3) it tells you that
> your people DID NOT appear in one of the listed periodicals thus
> allowing you to research elsewhere.[4]

This third statement is an interesting concept with regard to searching query indexes, as well as using other indexes. If an entry is not located in a particular index, this lack of information is still useful since it eliminates that index as a source for the problem being researched.

The final issue of QUERY NAME INDEX (January 1975) Indexes approximately 28,000 names. Mr. Colbert states that QNI has indexed approximately 200,000 personal names.[5] One hundred fifteen periodical titles are listed in the January 1975 issue of QNI, along with thirty-seven family organization newsletters and surname periodicals. It contains genealogical advertisements and other information of interest to genealogists.

Query Name Index

OLSEN, Ellen Marie DEN 62b

OLSON, Anna NOR MI 11) Mary Ann 62

O'NEAL, Silas NC SC, Mary SC, William Riley NC, Sarah, Bardin NC, Mary A. GA all MS, Edmond NC TX, Clarinda SC TX, Eli NC, Elizabeth SC, Barbara C, Savannah, Silas, Martha, Jane 9e) Mary Frances (Molly) TX, Aaron J, Caroline all AL, G.W. TX 80b

O'NEALE, William Turner, Eliza Virginia, Cloe E. 38

O'NEIL, James KS, Sadie Blanch MO KS 77

ONSTOTT, Abraham, Sarah, Mary A, Amelia A, Missouri A, Martha J. all MO TX 59

OPPENDICK-OPPENDYKE, Maria IL 122

ORCUTT, Olive 100b) Louise Caroline 115

ORDWAY, Mary, Bradshaw, Lucy 102b

O'REILLY, Catharine IRE 61b

OREM, William OH, Mary Ann OH 100b) William, Mary Ann, Sarah Elizabeth all OH 100e

ORME, Rebecca KY, Moses KY 92d

ORR, Sarah 9b) Christopher NC GA, Robert VA, Martha NC 9q) SAS 55b) John OH, Joshua OH 100e) Mary OH, Julia Ann OH 100e

ORRICK, Phillip P, Laura 22

ORTEN, William Nesbit, Samuel, Sarah all NC TN 119

ORTON, Edward KY, Anna KY 59) Edward KY 102) see Orten 119

ORTZ, Mary 74

ORVIS, Nancy 97

Fig. 15
Example from QUERY NAME INDEX,
vol. 3, no. 1, January 1975

OTHER QUERY INDEXES

In addition to the three query indexes already mentioned in this chapter, the following indexes are available in some libraries with a genealogical collection.[6]

Tilley, Risbrough Hammett, comp. THE AMERICAN GENEALOGICAL QUERIES. 2 vols. Newport, R.I.: R.H. Tilley, 1887, 1889.

> R.H. Tilley published a two-volume pamphlet containing genealogical queries. Even though the addresses in the queries are out of date, the genealogist may find clues since some of the basic genealogical data in the query will be unchanged--such as names, dates, places, relationships, and occupations. Also included in this work is an alphabetical listing of some of the earliest genealogical periodicals published in the United States and England. A short surname index to the queries in this pamphlet is included, as well as a few pages of genealogical advertisements. See Figure 16 for an example of this work.

Bierman, Edwinna Dodson, comp. THE SURNAME INDEX. San Gabriel, Calif.: 1962-66.

> In this publication, Bierman lists surnames which researchers are working on, along with the name and address of the researcher. Defining her purpose in preparing these indexes, she states in the preface, ". . . there is a definite need for a way to contact others who could help us and whom we could help in order to consolidate efforts and avoid duplication which is costly in time, effort and money. THE SURNAME INDEX is published for this purpose. Listings in the INDEX are accepted on the condition of free exchange of material."

> Each issue contains several sections, including one which lists surnames alphabetically and one which contains names and addresses of researchers interested in those surnames. In the surname section, usually just surnames are listed, but sometimes a state or country is shown with the surname. No specific research problems are indicated. A reference number is given in the surname section which is cross-referenced to the name and address of the person interested in that particular surname. Some of the addresses are obviously outdated. Nevertheless, this index may be useful in locating others working on the same surname. Most issues have separate sections which offer a variety of helpful research aids. A few titles from these sections are "Kinds of Queries, Their Limitations and Advantages"; "Answering Queries"; and "Writing Queries for Publication."

GENEALOGY & HISTORY, 1940-64. Published by Adrian Ely Mount and Bernice Wymond Mount, Washington, D.C. Quarterly. The serial is in vols. 1-14; the indexes are in vols. 1, 15-25. Publication discontinued.

BLOSS.—James[4] Bloss (Richard[3], Richard[2], Edmund[1],) born at Killingly, Conn., Nov. 3, 1702, died June 3, 1790. By his will recorded in Chepachet, R.I., proved Feb. 7, 1801, it appears that he was twice married, no mention being made of his first wife's name, and only the Christian name of his second being given, viz: Sarah. By his first wife he had I. Abigail, m. Sept. 30, 1749, John Younglove, afterwards, Sept. 13, 1770, m. Ebenezer Atwood. II, James III, Anne, m. 1759, Ephraim Ellingwood, of Woodstock. IV, John, m. March 9, 1758. Hannah Allen, of Pomfret. By his second wife his children were V. Ebenezer. VI, James, and VII, Job. I desire to obtain the names of the wives of James, Sr., with dates of marriage, also dates of birth of his children. James, Ebenezer. James 2d and Job.

123 Pearl Street, New York, N. Y.   JAMES O. BLOSS

Fig. 16
Example from THE AMERICAN
GENEALOGICAL QUERIES, 1887

The title page of each issue of GENEALOGY & HISTORY states
it is "the only periodical, of nationwide scope and circulation,
devoted to queries and answers relating to family history." Each
issue of this serial is replete with genealogical queries, answers
to queries, genealogical advertisements, and news items. The original format of the serial measures 11 1/2 x 16 inches but was
later reduced to 5 1/2 x 8 inches.

Beginning with volume 1, number 2, every item in this serial,
whether a query, advertisement, or article, includes an item number. Most of the indexes to this periodical refer to each item by
its item number, while a few of the indexes show the issue number,
page number, and column number where the entry can be found in
GENEALOGY & HISTORY. The indexes to GENEALOGY & HIS-
TORY are outlined below:

Volume 1: Indexes are at the end of vol. 1.
Volumes 2-14: Surname Index, vol. 15, no. 1, through vol. 17,
    no. 1; Geographical Index, vol. 17, nos. 1-3; Subject Index,
    vol. 17, no. 3.
All volumes: Comprehensive indexes, vol. 17, no. 4, through
    vol. 25, as follows:
    1. U.S. County Index, vol. 17, no. 4, through vol.
        18, no. 3. This index also includes areas smaller
        than counties. It consists of the county name and
        item number.
    2. U.S. Place Name Index, vol. 18, no. 3, through
        vol. 20, no. 4. This index largely duplicates the
        U.S. County Index, but is often easier to use since
        it consists of the place name and item number.
    3. Foreign Place Name Index, vol. 20, no. 4, through
        vol. 21, no. 1.
    4. Item-Writer's Residence Index, vol. 21, no. 1.
        This is primarily an index to queries, arranged by
        the state of residence of the inquirer.
    5. Writer's Item Number Index, vol. 21, no. 1,
        through vol. 21, no. 3. Arranged by inquirer's
        item number. Includes item numbers of responses
        to each query and serves as an index to these re-
        sponses.
    6. Index of Items with Full Name Signatures, vol. 21,
        no. 3. Primarily an index to advertisers in this
        serial.
    7. Index to Persons Cited in Items, vol. 21, no. 3,
        through vol. 22, no. 1. An index to living per-
        sons mentioned in the periodical, other than sub-
        mitters of queries.
    8. Bibliographical Index, vol. 22, no. 1, through
        vol. 23, no. 2. A list of the printed and manu-
        script works, librarians and libraries, and printers
        and publishers mentioned.

9. Topical Index, vol. 23, no. 3, through vol. 24,
   no. 3.
10. Indexes–Additions: Geographical, vol. 24, no. 3;
    Surname, vol. 24, no. 4.
11. Indexes–Corrections, vol. 24, no. 4.
12. Unnumbered Items, vol. 24, no. 4. Serves as an
    additional index to vol. 1, nos. 1 and 2.
13. Advertisements Index, vol. 24, no. 4, through vol.
    25, no. 4.
14. Late Additions, vol. 25, no. 4. Two pages of
    Advertisers, Persons Mentioned, Bibliographical,
    and Miscellaneous.

If a United States query included an ancestor's name, residence, and occupation, the query is indexed in the Surname Index, Geographical Index, U.S. County Index, U.S. Place Name Index, Item Writer's Index, and Topical Index (in the Topical Index, the query will be listed under the person's occupation). In spite of this duplication, all of the indexes contain information not found in the other indexes to GENEALOGY & HISTORY. The indexes show surnames, complete personal names, nicknames, locality entries, and subject headings (such as occupations, organizations, and religions).

GENEALOGY QUERIES. Independence, Mo.: Central States Mission, The Church of Jesus Christ of Latter–day Saints, 1959.

This query index contains thirty-four pages of genealogical queries typed alphabetically by the surname of the inquirer. Each entry is assigned a query number, such as A–10. The following Information is shown In each entry: item number, name and address of the inquirer (surname first in capitals), and genealogical query. A thirteen–page surname index is included as part of the work. This index shows the surname of the inquirer and surnames mentioned in each query, as well as the query number.

"Index to Queries," compiled by Rajahia Newton and Golden V. Adams, Jr. Logan, Utah: Cache Genealogical Library, 1960–62.

"Index to Queries" indexes surnames in queries found in many periodicals published in the United States and some foreign countries during the years 1960–62 which were received at the Cache Genealogical Library in Logan, Utah. A list of those periodicals which were indexed is included. Surnames are shown alphabetically along with the Cache Library call number, page number, name of publication, and date of issue. Volunteers at the Cache Genealogical Library assisted In preparing this index. "Index to Queries" has not been published. This indexing project has not been kept current. Other genealogical libraries may have similar indexing projects, in manuscript form or published locally.

NOTES

1. For a further explanation of how to use queries in genealogical research, see Edwinna Dodson Bierman's THE SURNAME INDEX (San Gabriel, Calif., 1966), and the DIRECTORY, GENEALOGICAL SOCIETIES AND PERIODICALS IN THE UNITED STATES, 1965 (San Gabriel, Calif., 1965).

2. THE AMERICAN GENEALOGIST 50 (1974): 125.

3. Letter, Mrs. Frank N. Reeder to Kip Sperry, 24 September 1974. Mrs. Reeder's address is 924 Solar Road, N.W., Albuquerque, New Mexico 87107.

4. QUERY NAME INDEX 2 (1974): 9. Publisher's address: Homestead Press, Drawer 220, Kenmore, Washington 98028.

5. Letter, Roy Colbert to Kip Sperry, 14 May 1974.

6. A short article on the advantages of placing queries is "What Coverage Can You Get?" THE SOUTHERNER 1 (1975): 67-68. This periodical is published by the Southern States Chapter, Utah Genealogical Association (P.O. Box 1144, Salt Lake City, Utah 84110). It lists the titles and addresses of nineteen newspapers which publish genealogical queries.

Chapter 10

USING COMPOSITE INDEXES

Selected examples showing the usefulness and importance of indexes to American genealogical periodicals are contained in this chapter. Six examples from composite genealogical periodical indexes are outlined, with corresponding entries from the periodicals indexed.

A general procedure for searching indexes to genealogical periodicals is to (1) look for the individual's full name, (2) look for that person's surname, including spelling variations, (3) check the localities of interest, then (4) look for other references in the index. The reader should refer to Chapter 3 for more information on this approach. After making note of the genealogical problem with regard to where the family resided, and also places of birth, marriage, death, and burial, one should check these pertinent localities in composite periodical indexes.

When looking for place names in indexes to periodicals, the researcher should use the direct locality approach (indexed by the smallest jurisdiction) and the indirect locality approach (such as the state or country, county, and town). Most composite periodical indexes carry cross-references, references to record sources, authors of articles, book reviews, and other data including personal names and place names.

If an entry of interest is located in the periodical index, an extract should be made of the information located, such as the name, type of record, periodical abbreviation, volume number, issue number, page numbers, and any other data shown. Next, one should obtain complete identification of the periodical title from the abbreviation used. A list of periodicals indexed might be included with the index, usually at the beginning of the index. The searcher should determine if the periodical is available at the library by checking the card catalog, serials holdings, or other bibliography. If the periodical is available, at a nearby library, he should then locate the pertinent volume and pages as shown in the index. If the periodical is not available at a local library, the user should check with other nearby libraries, consult with the reference librarian for a copy through interlibrary loan, or use the bibliographical sources included in Appendix 2.

The following are actual entries taken from periodical indexes and related genealogical periodicals. These examples were selected to illustrate the value of genealogical periodical literature and composite indexes. It is probable that more information about the names selected is available in other survey sources, such as family histories and local histories. Further information should be available in original records. These additional sources are not shown here since the purpose of this chapter is to illustrate the use of indexes to genealogical periodicals.

EXAMPLE I

OBJECTIVE: To use GENEALOGICAL PERIODICAL ANNUAL INDEX to locate an extract from a newspaper as published in a periodical.

A.   Assume one is looking for an ancestor, JONATHAN TUCKER of Cayuga County, New York, said to have died in 1822.

B.   As part of a search strategy the genealogist may wish to determine if there are any newspaper death notices in Jonathan's county of residence, Cayuga County, New York.

C.   After consulting GPAI, it was determined that there were no entries under this particular personal name. However, in the 1967 edition of GPAI (vol. 6) under the heading Cayuga County, New York, is the following (p. 37):

> "NEW YORK: Cayuga Co. death notices, newspapers, 1816-24 names Ro-Wh TT 7:1:24; 7:2:79; 7:3:132; 7:4:187"

D.   The periodical reference in the preface to GPAI shows "TT" as "Tree Talks, Central N.Y.G.S., Box 104, Colvin Station, Syracuse, N.Y. 13205."

E.   The searcher should next locate volume 7 (1967) of TREE TALKS. The following is found in volume 7, number 3, page 132:

> "Deaths 1816-1824 from AUBURN GAZETTE and CAYUGA REPUBLICAN, both published Wednesdays in Auburn, New York. . . . TUCKER, Jonathan, aged 60 yrs., died Sat. night on 13th inst. at Pratt's Tavern, 12 mi. this side of Albany. Mr. J. T. of this village. He was returning from Albany with a loaded waggon. His disorder was an inflammation on the lungs. (Cay. Rep. July 17, 1822)"

NOTE: Further research is needed to confirm that this is the Jonathan Tucker of interest.

EXAMPLE II

OBJECTIVE: To use GENEALOGICAL PERIODICAL ANNUAL INDEX to locate an extract of a marriage record published in a periodical.

A.   Assume a genealogist is looking for a marriage record for WILLIAM

BLACK and CATHERINE WANEY said to have been married in or near LIVINGSTON COUNTY, NEW YORK, in 1849.

B. After consulting GPAI, it was determined that there were no entries for these particular individuals. In the 1968 edition of GPAI (vol. 7) under this locality heading is the following (p. 37):

> "NEW YORK: Livingston Co., Conesus marr recs 1848–1849 TT 8:1:34"

C. The periodical reference in the front of GPAI shows "TT" as "Tree Talks, Central N.Y. Gen. Soc., Box 104, Colvin Station, Syracuse, NY 13205."

D. After locating volume 8 (1968) of TREE TALKS, the following is found in volume 8, number 1, March 1968, page 34:

> "Vital Records of New York State, Livingston County Courthouse, Geneseo, N.Y. . . . Marriages in Town of Conesus, 1849. . . . William Black, 34, of Geneseo, to Catherine Waney, 24, of Groveland, by James A. Mc Kay, Esq., September 30, 1849."

EXAMPLE III

OBJECTIVE: To use GENEALOGICAL PERIODICAL ANNUAL INDEX to locate a family history in a periodical.

A. Assume a researcher is looking for family information for JOHN BOYD, born about 1780. John married ELIZABETH LEATH about 1800. They resided in ANDERSON COUNTY, TENNESSEE.

B. After consulting GPAI, it was determined that there was no entry for a John Boyd indexed separately. However, the following entry was located under the BOYD SURNAME In the 1969 edition of GPAI (vol. 8), page 6:

> "BOYD, William (b 1761) w Mary Wasson & Nancy Small, N.C., Tenn., Ala., Rev pens claim abst; son John (b 1777) w Elizabeth Leath; family – TAN 16:2:61"

C. The periodical reference in the front of GPAI shows "TAN" as "Tennessee Gen. Soc., Ansearchin' News, P.O. Box 12124, Memphis, TN 38112."

D. Next the reader needs to locate ANSEARCHIN' NEWS, volume 16, number 2, April–June 1969, pages 61–66, family history of the Boyd family entitled "William Boyd." The following excerpt is shown from this family history:

> ". . . William Boyd, a son of George Boyd, was born in Orange Co., N.C. on March 15, 1761. His first wife was Mary Wasson. He had two sons by Mary Wasson––Henry S. Boyd and John Boyd. . . . John Boyd, born in North Carolina, Dec. 9, 1777, and Elizabeth Leath, born in Virginia, Aug. 29, 1785, were married in Anderson County, Tennessee Dec. 16, 1801. . . ."

NOTE: The compiler of this family history used these sources for this compilation: a certified copy of the Bible record of John and Elizabeth (Leath) Boyd,
a local history, military and pension records, and a court record. Boyd descendants are shown in this periodical article.

EXAMPLE IV

OBJECTIVE: To use Jacobus's INDEX TO GENEALOGICAL PERIODICALS to
locate a family history in a periodical.

A. Assume one is looking for family information on an ancestor, JO-
    CHEM CALJER, who married MAGDALENT JE WAELE. They were
    members of the Reformed Dutch Church in New Amsterdam, New
    York, in the 1640s.
B. The following was a result of searches in Jacobus's indexes:
    1. Volume 1: No references to Caljer and similar spellings.
    2. Volume 2: The following entry was located on page 16:
        "Colyer [Caljer], Jòchem; New York; B4 (20–97)."
C. The periodical reference in front of Jacobus's index shows "B4" as
    THE AMERICAN GENEALOGIST.
D. After locating THE AMERICAN GENEALOGIST, volume 20, num-
    ber 2, October 1943, the Colyer family is shown on pages 97–
    105:

> "The Colyer Family of Long Island," by Herbert F.
> Seversmith. "The first ancestor of this family appears
> in New Amsterdam, New Netherlands, shortly prior to
> 9 March 1642, when he brought a son to be baptised
> in the Reformed Dutch church in Manhattan. . . . The
> church record calls him Jochem Kayker in 1642."

NOTE: This article contains references to several sources, including church
records. It continues by describing Jochem Caljer.

EXAMPLE V

OBJECTIVE: To use Jacobus's INDEX TO GENEALOGICAL PERIODICALS to
locate cemetery records published in a periodical.

A. Assume one is looking for an ancestor, NATHANIEL BROCKWAY,
    who died in 1838, in or near CANAAN, COLUMBIA COUNTY,
    NEW YORK. His wife was SILVAH BROCKWAY.
B. After consulting Jacobus's periodical indexes, no entry for this name
    was located in the personal name indexes. However, the following
    entry was found in volume 1 in the "Place Index" section:

> "Canaan, Columbia County, N.Y., Inscriptions;
> M(18–65)."
> Note the direct locality entry.

C. The periodical reference in front of Jacobus's index shows "M" as
    the NATIONAL GENEALOGICAL SOCIETY QUARTERLY.

D.   After locating the NATIONAL GENEALOGICAL SOCIETY QUAR-
     TERLY, volume 18, number 3, September 1930, tombstone inscrip-
     tions are shown on pages 65–68:

> "Tombstone Inscriptions, Canaan Cemetery, Columbia
> County, N.Y. . . . . Natl. Brockway, died Sept. 7,
> 1838, Ag. 90 y. 5 m. 4 d. 'The sweet remembrance
> of the just shall flourish though they sleep in dust.'
> Silvah, wife of Natl. Brockway, died Mch. 23, 1834,
> age 83 yrs., 4 m., 24 d."

EXAMPLE VI

OBJECTIVE: To use Munsell's INDEX TO AMERICAN GENEALOGIES to locate
a family genealogy published in a periodical.

A.   Assume one is looking for family information for ABRAHAM BIN-
     INGER, born in 1720 in Switzerland, who was married to MARTHA
     MARINER.   Family sources state this family lived in New York
     and Pennsylvania during the middle 1700s.
B.   After consulting Munsell's INDEX TO AMERICAN GENEALOGIES,
     no reference to the Bininger surname was located in the 5th edition.
     However, the following was located in Munsell's SUPPLEMENT 1900
     TO 1908 TO THE INDEX TO GENEALOGIES PUBLISHED IN 1900,
     page 11:

> "Bininger – N.Y. Gen. and Biog. Rec., xxxiii, 135-7."

C.   After locating THE NEW YORK GENEALOGICAL AND BIOGRAPHI-
     CAL RECORD, volume 33, number 3, July 1902, the following is
     an abstract from the article on pages 135-37, entitled "Abraham
     Bininger," by John B. Pine:

> This article mentions Abraham Bininger's immigration to
> the United States from Bulock (or Baden-Bulach) in Can-
> ton Zurich, Switzerland, where he was born 18 January
> 1720.   On 16 October 1746 he married Martha Mariner
> at Bethlehem.   Other information is contained in this
> article including information about their children.

SUMMARY

Only a few illustrations from composite genealogical periodical indexes have
been shown in this chapter.   Other states, regions, and record sources are represented in indexes to genealogical periodicals.

Users of these indexes will need to be alert to all possible surnames for the
problem of interest, spelling variations, and all possible references to place
names.   Additional information might be available in genealogical periodicals
after an article was published.   Sometimes additions and corrections are published in the same or another periodical.

Using Composite Indexes

After locating an article of interest, the genealogist should verify the information located by searching in other sources. Whenever possible, one should locate original records and printed sources which are documented in order to verify that which is printed in periodicals.

Chapter 11

EPILOGUE

This book has attempted to demonstrate that indexes to genealogical periodicals are an important source and should not be overlooked by researchers. These indexes should be systematically searched as part of one's research methodology.

There are three general types of indexes to genealogical periodicals:

1. Composite indexes
2. Indexes to each periodical (individual periodical titles)
   a. Cumulative indexes
   b. Indexes to each issue or volume
3. Special indexes, such as query indexes

A three-step approach is recommended when using these indexes: (1) search composite periodical indexes first, beginning with the most recent issues published, working backwards to the earliest indexes, (2) search indexes to individual serial publications--especially those published in the area(s) of the research problem, and (3) search query indexes for references to the name(s) of interest to the genealogist. As part of step three, one should also search other specialized periodical indexes.

An example of a survey calendar which lists titles of composite periodical indexes is included as Appendix 4. This may prove helpful for the genealogist while he is working on a pedigree problem.

Due to the complexities and incompleteness of the composite indexes to American genealogical periodicals described in this book, one must consider the fact that a comprehensive search of these sources is often time consuming and tedious. Some searches may not be worth the effort expended. As an example, one will likely not find names of modern immigrants among the pages of genealogical periodicals and indexes to said periodicals. A single comprehensive index to this literature is not available at this time.

Epilogue

ACCESS TO TITLES OF PERIODICALS

Once a selected item is located in a composite periodical index such as GENE-
ALOGICAL PERIODICAL ANNUAL INDEX, how does the researcher locate the
particular issue of that serial mentioned in the composite index? This problem
can be approached through one of these solutions to this question:

1. The periodical of interest might be available in the same library
    where the composite index is housed. This could be a genealogical,
    public, or academic library.
2. The periodical may be available at a nearby library which houses
    genealogical periodicals.
3. A photocopy of the particular article or serial might be available
    through interlibrary loan, although serials are usually not circulated.
    Photoduplicated copies of serials or a particular article are often
    available for a nominal fee. The interested genealogist will need
    to contact a public or academic library which participates in inter-
    library loan for further information concerning this service.
4. A photocopy of the article of interest might be available by writing
    directly to the library housing the serial title.[1]
5. If the researcher is near one of the many branch genealogical li-
    braries of the Genealogical Society, a "Branch Genealogical Li-
    brary Reference Questionnaire" is available for requesting copies
    of materials from the main library in Salt Lake City. A nominal
    photocopying fee is charged for this service.[2]

HOUSING GENEALOGICAL INDEXES

Libraries with a genealogical collection should keep composite periodical indexes on a register table, index table, or beside other composite and specialized
indexes. This will provide easy access for patrons of the library as well as reference personnel. Making these readily accessible will facilitate their use.
It will also prevent these sources from becoming "buried" in the stacks or reference area.

Libraries should maintain a standing order for GENEALOGICAL PERIODICAL
ANNUAL INDEX and should consider subscribing to the TOPICAL INDEX OF
GENEALOGICAL QUARTERLIES. Libraries with only a few genealogical sources
should as a minimum subscribe to GPAI. Patrons can gain access to genealogical data hidden in periodicals by using these composite indexes. Important
titles of American genealogical periodicals are shown with an asterisk in appendix 3. Genealogical libraries should subscribe to the best genealogical
and historical periodicals available.

Librarians should place appropriate cards in their card catalog so researchers
can locate references to these important composite indexes and periodical titles.
A separate handout listing these indexes, periodical titles, and their library
call numbers may prove useful. It is frustrating to genealogists when these
titles are inaccessible, either by their physical arrangement or the arrangement
of cards in the card catalog.

There is a need for instruction in the use of indexes to genealogical periodicals. Reference sections of libraries housing these indexes could perform a needed educational function by instructing researchers on how to make effective use of indexes to genealogical periodical literature. Instruction could be accomplished by classes, handouts, self-learning units, and other reference assistance.

THE AUTHOR'S STUDY OF BIBLIOGRAPHICAL CONTROL

As a partial requirement for a Master's degree in Library and Information Sciences, the author wrote a project entitled "A Study of Bibliographical Control of United States Genealogical Periodical Literature."[3] As part of this study, a questionnaire was mailed to Certified Genealogists and United States Accredited Genealogists. The instrument was designed to measure the attitudes of these two groups of professional genealogists with regard to the problem of bibliographical control of American genealogical periodicals.

Of the genealogists who responded to this questionnaire, it was found that many of them used AYER DIRECTORY OF PUBLICATIONS as a source for locating bibliographical information pertaining to United States genealogical periodicals. A number of respondents seldom used Munsell's INDEX TO AMERICAN GENEALOGIES, Jacobus's INDEX TO GENEALOGICAL PERIODICALS, and GENEALOGICAL PERIODICAL ANNUAL INDEX. The lack of use of these three indexes may be due to one or more of the following:

1. The genealogists lacked confidence in the results obtained from searching periodical indexes
2. The genealogists were not well informed concerning the use of indexes to genealogical periodicals
3. The indexes to genealogical periodicals were not available
4. The periodical indexes were too complicated to use

The respondents to the questionnaire felt there were a variety of deficiencies in the available indexes to United States genealogical periodicals. A summary of these deficiencies, according to an analysis of the data, follows:

1. Many genealogical and historical periodicals are omitted from the available periodical indexes
2. A cumulative index to genealogical periodicals does not exist
3. Periodicals included in the indexes are only partially indexed
4. Too few subject headings are used in the indexing of genealogical periodicals
5. Periodical indexes are divided into separate volumes, making it necessary to search each one individually
6. Munsell's INDEX TO AMERICAN GENEALOGIES indexes only surnames
7. Jacobus's INDEX TO GENEALOGICAL PERIODICALS contains eleven sections in three separate volumes which must be searched individually
8. Recent indexes (1970-73) to GENEALOGICAL PERIODICAL ANNUAL INDEX are not available for searching [as of 1977]

The majority of responding genealogists felt they would like to have genealogical periodicals indexed by surnames and by given names. A number of respondents also indicated they would like the periodicals indexed by localities in the articles, and also by subject headings.

AMERICAN LIBRARY ASSOCIATION, "PROSPECTUS"

The Genealogy Committee of the History Section of the American Library Association (ALA) met in 1968 to discuss an ambitious proposal to index genealogical and historical periodicals. They realized a comprehensive index to all articles in genealogical and historical periodicals would be a tremendous asset to genealogists. It was envisioned by this committee that every journal of a genealogical or heraldic nature, and any other journal containing a reasonable amount of genealogy, would be indexed by volunteers, librarians, and genealogists. Their proposed index would begin with the year 1845 and continue through 1970 or later. Even book reviews of more than half a page would be indexed.

A trial index to ten United States genealogical periodicals was prepared by the ALA Genealogy Committee. This trial index contains about 500 entries and is entitled PROSPECTUS: CUMULATIVE INDEX TO WRITINGS IN AMERICAN GENEALOGICAL PERIODICALS, 1845-1970.[4]

Because of insufficient funds and lack of interest, the ALA indexing project has not begun. Perhaps ALA should consider regional indexing projects, since these might be more efficiently managed. The indexes obtained from regional projects could later be combined into a national cumulative index. Genealogical and historical societies should cooperate with ALA in this indexing. A united effort could result in a cumulative index to American genealogical and historical periodicals. There is a great need for a retrospective and comprehensive index to American genealogical periodicals.

THE FUTURE

Because it is the most recent and complete index to genealogical periodicals published in North America, GENEALOGICAL PERIODICAL ANNUAL INDEX must be kept current. It should be expanded in both scope and comprehensiveness to include all significant genealogical items in periodicals and all relevant materials in related fields, especially history. GPAI should be enlarged to include all major genealogical periodicals published in the United States, Canada, and Great Britain.

Other English-language periodicals should also be considered for inclusion in GPAI. It should index articles in more depth to include additional entries for personal names not now being indexed. More in-depth subject (topical) headings should be used, especially for articles concerning techniques and research methodology. The compiler of GPAI should subscribe to serials not donated for indexing, or visit genealogical libraries to obtain needed issues.

It is time for genealogists, librarians, historians, indexers, editors, and computer programmers to work together to exchange indexing methods and information. All possible uses of computer technology for retrieval of relevant genealogical and historical data from records should be explored. Aside from personal names, the scholarly researcher needs access to occupations, ages, localities, and relationships. Computers have the capabilities of giving genealogists the information needed to locate individuals and help extend pedigrees.

NOTES

1. The researcher should be aware of any possible violations of the copyright law when requesting photocopies of serials or other materials. Some libraries are hesitant to photocopy material under copyright; others will provide the requested copies. Some libraries stamp the photocopies, stating they are under copyright and are for personal use only.

2. One can determine the nearest LDS branch genealogical library by writing to the Genealogical Society, 50 East North Temple, Salt Lake City, Utah 84150, or by checking a telephone directory.

3. Kip Sperry, "A Study of Bibliographical Control of United States Genealogical Periodical Literature," Master's project, Brigham Young University, Provo, Utah, 1974. This project is available at the Harold B. Lee Library, Brigham Young University, Provo, Utah; the Genealogical Society Library, Salt Lake City, Utah (on microfilm); and the National Genealogical Society Library, Washington, D.C.

4. American Library Association, Genealogy Committee, PROSPECTUS: CUMULATIVE INDEX TO WRITINGS IN AMERICAN GENEALOGICAL PERIODICALS, 1845-1970 (Chicago: American Library Association, 1973). This trial index is appended to the author's MLS field project cited in note 3.

Appendix 1

OTHER GENEALOGICAL PERIODICAL INDEXES

Incorporated in this appendix is an annotated bibliography of indexes to genealogical periodicals and bibliographies. These works usually cover more than
one state or subject, or provide access to more than one genealogical periodical title. The composite periodical indexes which were described earlier in
this book, Munsell, Jacobus, GPAI, etc., are not repeated here.

The intent of this appendix is to bring to light little-used and little-known
titles, as well as popular works which index--or partially index--American
genealogical periodicals. These sources will be of interest to American genealogists. Important bibliographic titles which cite articles from genealogical
periodicals are also included, since these provide limited access to periodical
literature.

AMERICA: HISTORY AND LIFE. Santa Barbara, Calif.: American Bibliographical Center, Clio Press, Vol. 1, no. 1, July 1964-- . Annual.

This set of volumes indexes historical and some genealogical periodicals of in-
terest to United States and Canadian genealogists. It is the major guide to
American historical periodical literature. Entries include brief abstracts. Shows
reference in early volumes to abstracting and indexing such titles as THE
GENEALOGICAL HELPER and THE GENEALOGICAL MAGAZINE OF NEW
JERSEY, along with many historical titles.

Indexes divided into parts: part A contains article abstracts and citations;
part B, indexes to book reviews; part C, American history bibliography; and
part D, annual index.

American Library Association. Genealogy Committee. PROSPECTUS: CUMU-
LATIVE INDEX TO WRITINGS IN AMERICAN GENEALOGICAL PERIODICALS,
1845-1970. Chicago: American Library Association, 1973.

This eleven-page pamphlet is a trial index of selected entries from
the following ten selected genealogical periodicals for the year
1970:

THE LOUISIANA GENEALOGICAL REGISTER
THE MARYLAND AND DELAWARE GENEALOGIST
MARYLAND GENEALOGICAL SOCIETY BULLETIN
THE DETROIT SOCIETY FOR GENEALOGICAL RE-
SEARCH MAGAZINE
THE NEW ENGLAND HISTORICAL AND GENEALOGI-
CAL REGISTER
NATIONAL GENEALOGICAL SOCIETY QUARTERLY
THE NEW YORK GENEALOGICAL AND BIOGRAPHICAL
RECORD
GATEWAY TO THE WEST
OREGON END OF THE TRAIL RESEARCHER
SEATTLE GENEALOGICAL SOCIETY BULLETIN

The trial index to these serials is found on pages 5-11 in this
PROSPECTUS. The entries are alphabetically arranged by surnames,
localities, and subjects. Index entries are capitalized, making the
index easy to use. Full bibliographic data are given so the user
can easily locate information about the serial of interest. Only
1970 issues were indexed.

The periodical indexing project envisioned by this committee has
never materialized, probably because of the extreme cost of the
project and the lack of interest from professional genealogists and
librarians. This PROSPECTUS will be difficult to locate, since it
is not readily available in most libraries with a genealogical collection. See chapter 11 for further reference.

Banks, Charles Edward. TOPOGRAPHICAL DICTIONARY OF 2885 ENGLISH
EMIGRANTS TO NEW ENGLAND, 1620-1650. 1937. Reprint. Baltimore:
Genealogical Publishing Co., 1963.

This work partially indexes five genealogical periodicals. Titles
are abbreviated in a column entitled "Various Reference." Although this work may prove helpful in finding the locality of residence of a New England immigrant, it is very incomplete. The
book is well indexed.

Beers, Henry Putney. BIBLIOGRAPHIES IN AMERICAN HISTORY: GUIDE TO
MATERIALS FOR RESEARCH. 1942. Reprint. New York: Octagon Books,
1973.

Contains comprehensive bibliographies and a chapter entitled "Biography and Genealogy." Includes some entries from genealogical
and other periodicals. This bibliography is well indexed.

CATALOGUE OF THE GENEALOGICAL AND HISTORICAL LIBRARY OF THE
COLONIAL DAMES OF THE STATE OF NEW YORK. New York: Historical
Society of the Colonial Dames of America, 1912. Reprint. Ann Arbor: Gry-
phon Books, 1971.

This work acts as a surname index to several genealogical periodicals. It indexes subjects and localities. Lists family genealogies in some periodicals.

THE CHRISTIAN-EVANGELIST INDEX, 1863-1958. 3 vols. St. Louis, Mo.: Published jointly by the Christian Board of Publication and Disciples of Christ Historical Society, Nashville, Tennessee, 1962.

Although not genealogically oriented, this set indexes five Christian magazines available on microfilm from the Disciples of Christ Historical Society, Nashville, Tennessee. An author, subject, and book review index, it also indexes countless obituaries.

CIVIL WAR INDEX. 13 vols. Chicago: Joseph A. Huebner; River Grove, Ill.: Russell L. Knor, 1956-68.

A personal name, subject, and locality index to Civil War literature. Indexes some periodicals.

Colket, Meredith B., Jr. FOUNDERS OF EARLY AMERICAN FAMILIES: EMIGRANTS FROM EUROPE, 1607-1657. Cleveland: General Court of the Order of Founders and Patriots of America, 1975.

This work is a partial index to male colonists appearing in various sources, including a few genealogical periodicals, such as THE AMERICAN GENEALOGIST. As Colket states in the preface to this work, "This study represents an effort to comb the most appropriate genealogical literature pertaining to the early colonists and their descendants, to evaluate the literature and to select and cite the best authorities."

Crozier, William Armstrong. A KEY TO SOUTHERN PEDIGREES. 2d ed. Baltimore: Southern Book Co., 1953.

This eighty-page work indexes surnames only. The lengthy subtitle indicates this is "a comprehensive guide to the Colonial ancestry of families in the states of Virginia, Maryland, Georgia, North Carolina, South Carolina, Kentucky, Tennessee, West Virginia and Alabama." A few major genealogical periodicals are indexed. Only volume numbers are shown.

CUMULATED MAGAZINE SUBJECT INDEX, 1907-1949. 2 vols. Boston: G.K. Hall & Co., 1964.

A composite photographic reproduction of the entries as they were originally printed in forty-three volumes of the ANNUAL MAGAZINE SUBJECT INDEX, edited by Frederick Winthrop Faxon, 1907-35; Mary E. Bates, 1936-44; and Anne C. Sutherland, 1942-49 (published by the F.W. Faxon Company, 1907-49). This 2-volume reproduction indexes a variety of historical, and several genealogical, titles of interest to American genealogists. Six examples of titles indexed and the years covered are:

ANNALS OF IOWA, 1907-15; 1920-49
THE 'OLD NORTHWEST' GENEALOGICAL QUARTERLY,
1907-12
THE PENNSYLVANIA MAGAZINE OF HISTORY AND
BIOGRAPHY, 1908-49
THE SOUTH CAROLINA HISTORICAL AND GENEA-
LOGICAL MAGAZINE, vols. 8-50, 1907-49
THE UTAH GENEALOGICAL AND HISTORICAL MAGA-
ZINE, 1918-40
WILLIAM AND MARY COLLEGE QUARTERLY, 1921-49

Draughon, Wallace R., and Johnson, William Perry, comps. NORTH CARO-
LINA GENEALOGICAL REFERENCE. 2d ed. Durham, N.C.: Seeman Printery,
1966.

Indexes families in some genealogical periodicals in a section entitled, "Printed Genealogies and Family Histories." Many North
Carolina families are shown in this section, but they do not per-
tain exclusively to families from this state.

Filby, P. William, comp. AMERICAN & BRITISH GENEALOGY & HERALDRY:
A SELECTED LIST OF BOOKS. 2d ed. Chicago: American Library Association, 1975.

The introduction to this extensive bibliography states it includes
"definitive articles of some length which have appeared in the
leading genealogical and historical journals." Filby does not include a separate list of serials which have been cited in this bibliography. It serves as a type of index to some of the major genealogical periodicals. For the articles included, this work shows
the name of the author of the article (if any), title of the article,
title of the periodical, volume number, and year. This bibliography does not, however, index all important periodical articles
published in North America and Britain. For those indexed, most
entries are annotated. An excellent index concludes this book.
This is an outstanding reference work.

Flavell, Carol Willsey, comp. OHIO GENEALOGICAL PERIODICAL INDEX:
A COUNTY GUIDE. Youngstown, Ohio: Carol Willsey Flavell, 1977.

An index to periodical articles pertaining to the state of Ohio.
Arranged by counties. Indexes a variety of genealogical periodicals. Family names are not indexed, but shows references to Ohio
records found in genealogical periodicals.

Forbes, Harriette Merrifield, comp. NEW ENGLAND DIARIES, 1602-1800.
Topsfield, Mass.: privately printed, 1923.

An annotated catalog of New England diaries, orderly books, and

sea journals. Shows references to some diaries published in genealogical periodicals, as well as other publications. An important
source for New England genealogists.

THE GRAFTON INDEX OF THE TITLES OF BOOKS AND MAGAZINE ARTI-
CLES ON HISTORY, GENEALOGY AND BIOGRAPHY PRINTED IN THE UNI-
TED STATES ON AMERICAN SUBJECTS DURING THE YEAR 1909. New York:
Grafton Press, 1910.

Partially indexes seventy-four magazines--popular, historical, and
genealogical--for the year 1909 only. No more issues of this index were published. A personal name, subject, and locality index,
it has sixty-eight pages. Not comprehensive, but could prove
helpful in locating early published locality records or family genealogies. Arranged in one alphabet, although originally published
quarterly.

Griffin, Appleton Prentiss Clark. BIBLIOGRAPHY OF AMERICAN HISTORICAL
SOCIETIES. ANNUAL REPORT OF THE AMERICAN HISTORICAL ASSOCIA-
TION FOR THE YEAR 1905, vol. 2, 2d ed., rev. and enl. 1907. Reprint.
Detroit: Gale Research, 1966.

A 1,030-page bibliography of historical sources complemented by
342 pages of indexes. These include subject and author index,
biographical index, and index of societies. Publications of genealogical and biographical societies are among the pages of bibliog-
raphies--as are historical societies. Contents of some of these pub
lications are then outlined and included in the extensive indexes.
Genealogies are included. This work is helpful in locating early
published historical and genealogical sources before 1906.

_____. INDEX OF THE LITERATURE OF AMERICAN LOCAL HISTORY IN
COLLECTIONS PUBLISHED IN 1890-95. Boston: Carl H. Heintzemann, 1896.

A locality index to published records in 140 early historical and
genealogical publications including periodicals. Volume and beginning page number are shown for each entry in this 151-page
index. Indexes many published vital records and family information under each locality heading (states, counties, towns, regions,
and other place names).

Haverford College. Library. QUAKER NECROLOGY. 2 vols. Boston:
G.K. Hall, 1961.

QUAKER NECROLOGY contains approximately 59,000 entries from
four Quaker periodicals in the obituary card index file of the
Quaker Collection at the Haverford College Library. The index
was begun ca. 1922 and continued to 1960. Both Orthodox and
Hicksite Quakers (Society of Friends) have been indexed in this
file. Each entry refers to deaths of Quakers for the time period
ca. 1828 to 1960. Although not all Quakers have been included,

many have been indexed; therefore, this work is useful in locating biographies and death notices of Quakers. Each entry in this necrology shows the individual's name, title of the publication, volume and page numbers and year. Entries are alphabetically arranged by surname.

This index is helpful in locating genealogical information for Quakers who died in North America during the years indexed. It is an important index to Quakers. The following four Quaker periodicals are indexed in QUAKER NECROLOGY:

THE FRIEND
FRIENDS' WEEKLY INTELLIGENCER (title varied)
THE AMERICAN FRIEND (formerly THE FRIENDS' RE-
VIEW and thè CHRISTIAN WORKER)
FRIENDS JOURNAL (formerly THE FRIEND and FRIENDS'
INTELLIGENCER)

Helmbold, F. Wilbur. TRACING YOUR ANCESTRY: A STEP-BY-STEP GUIDE TO RESEARCHING YOUR FAMILY HISTORY. Birmingham, Ala.: Oxmoor House, 1976.

A listing of some articles from genealogical periodicals is included in the bibliography to this introductory text. Also included is a bibliography of United States genealogical periodicals, although it is incomplete. This text will be especially useful to those who are beginning their American research. Illustrated.

Hostetler, John A. ANNOTATED BIBLIOGRAPHY ON THE AMISH. Scottdale, Pa.: Mennonite Publishing House, 1951.

An annotated bibliography of references concerning Amish Men-nonites. Has references to articles in periodical literature. Con-tains a map showing the location of old order Amish Mennonite communities in the United States.

"Illinois Periodical Index". In: ILLINOIS STATE GENEALOGICAL SOCIETY QUARTERLY. Vol. 1, no. 1, April 1969-- . Annual.

An annual article appearing in the first issues for each year of the ILLINOIS STATE GENEALOGICAL SOCIETY QUARTERLY. These indexes serve as surname and subject indexes to the key genea-logical periodicals published in Illinois. Locality records are also indexed. This is an excellent composite index to Illinois genea-logical serials. The index begins with volume 1, number 1, April 1969.

INDEX TO THE WRITINGS ON AMERICAN HISTORY, 1902-1940. Washing-ton, D.C.: American Historical Association, 1956.

An extensive 1,115-page index to family surnames, localities, and subject (topical) headings. Surnames and complete personal names are indexed. Indexes the valuable set WRITINGS ON AMERICAN HISTORY. Genealogists should not overlook this important index or collection.

Jacobus, Donald Lines. "Index to Genealogical Periodicals." THE AMERICAN GENEALOGIST 9-23 (1933-47).

Published as INDEX TO GENEALOGICAL PERIODICALS. See Chapter 5, above, for further reference.

Libby, Charles Thornton. GENEALOGICAL DICTIONARY OF MAINE AND NEW HAMPSHIRE. Portland: Southworth Press, 1928.

Prior to the dictionary portion of this work, under a section entitled "Lists," Libby's DICTIONARY partially indexes some New England sources, including THE NEW ENGLAND HISTORICAL AND GENEALOGICAL REGISTER. This section of Libby's DICTIONARY serves as a partial index to some Maine and New Hampshire locality records.

Long Island Historical Society. Library. CATALOGUE OF AMERICAN GENE-ALOGIES IN THE LIBRARY OF THE LONG ISLAND HISTORICAL SOCIETY. Prepared under the direction of Emma Toedteberg. Brooklyn: Long Island Historical Society, 1935.

This 660-page work is a surname reference only but includes some entries showing published genealogies in genealogical periodicals. Mostly a family history index for the major surname in family histories.

Miller, Olga K. MIGRATION, EMIGRATION, IMMIGRATION: PRINCIPALLY TO THE UNITED STATES AND IN THE UNITED STATES. Logan, Utah: Everton Publishers, 1974.

This monumental work is a bibliography of sources arranged by subjects and localities. States of the United States are arranged alphabetically and many foreign countries are included. It is a collection of numerous references to printed sources concerning the subject of migration, emigration, and immigration to and within the United States. Miller includes important references concerning this subject from many genealogical and historical periodicals. The appendix lists 290 American and foreign serial titles which are mentioned in this bibliography. This work is useful in locating sources containing lists of persons and works dealing with this subject. Indexed.

Newberry Library. Chicago. THE GENEALOGICAL INDEX. 4 vols. Boston: G.K. Hall, 1960.

This is a popular index of surnames to selected historical and genealogical periodicals, compilations, biographical works, local histories, and other sources in the collections of the Newberry Library in Chicago. Each volume consists of photographic reproductions of an analytical index prepared at the Newberry Library. Many of the sources indexed are available in other genealogical libraries, however.

This index is especially useful in pinpointing surnames, particularly uncommon surnames, and is an important finding tool. It can be used to identify a surname in a specific state or locality. The index was begun in 1896 but was discontinued during World War I, and has not been kept current. It contains over a million entries.

Surnames are alphabetically arranged and thereunder are grouped by sections: United States general, regions (such as New England), states of the United States (listed alphabetically), and allied families. Many surnames are also listed alphabetically under names of foreign countries. This is mostly an index to United States sources, however.

Complete titles or abbreviated titles of published sources are shown in each entry, along with the year of publication, and often volume number and page number. The Newberry Library call number is also given with each entry. Some "see" references are included, referring the reader from one surname to another. Sometimes the indexed surname has been taken from a biographical sketch. Other references may only be to a brief mention of that surname in the source indexed.

Users must be aware that this is a surname index only. It will be difficult to identify common surnames, except those from a particular state or region. Most titles are abbreviated and may appear cryptic to the average reader. Not all the references can be found in libraries other than the Newberry Library.

Passano, Eleanor Phillips. AN INDEX OF THE SOURCE RECORDS OF MARYLAND: GENEALOGICAL, BIOGRAPHICAL, HISTORICAL. 1940. Reprint. Baltimore: Genealogical Publishing Co., 1967.

This work is divided into several sections, the important ones being the personal name index, locality index, and genealogy index. References to periodical articles from magazines are given. Although this book indexes mostly Maryland sources, it is not limited to this state only. An excellent finding aid.

Reed, Henry Clay, and Reed, Marion Bjornson, comps. A BIBLIOGRAPHY OF DELAWARE THROUGH 1960. Newark: University of Delaware Press, 1966.

Includes an excellent bibliography of titles dealing with Delaware biography and family history. Some of the entries are references to articles in genealogical periodicals. An excellent finding aid for the Delaware historian and genealogist. Bibliographic entries are not alphabetically arranged. Only includes material published through the year 1960. Indexed.

Rider, Fremont, ed. THE AMERICAN GENEALOGICAL INDEX. 1st series,
48 vols. Middletown, Conn., 1942-51. THE AMERICAN GENEALOGICAL-
BIOGRAPHICAL INDEX. 2d series, in process. Middletown, Conn.: Godfrey
Memorial Library, 1952-- .

> Although this extensive collection indexes mostly published vital
> and church records, family and local histories, the 1790 census,
> revolutionary war records, and the BOSTON TRANSCRIPT, both
> series give reference to indexing THE NORTH CAROLINA HIS-
> TORICAL AND GENEALOGICAL REGISTER, 1900-1903. The
> second series includes reference to three genealogical periodical
> titles. One would not, however, normally use this collection
> to locate references in genealogical periodicals.

Rubincam, Milton. GENEALOGY: A SELECTED BIBLIOGRAPHY. Prepared
for the Institute of Genealogy, Samford University. Birmingham, Ala.: Banner
Press, 1967. Additions and corrections, 1970.

> This twenty-page pamphlet includes some references to articles in
> American genealogical periodicals. Not comprehensive.

St. Louis, Missouri. Public Library. GENEALOGICAL MATERIAL AND LO-
CAL HISTORIES IN THE ST. LOUIS PUBLIC LIBRARY. Rev. ed. by George
Gambrill. St. Louis: 1965.

> This publication indexes various articles found in genealogical,
> historical, and other periodicals. Entries are listed by author or
> title. Incomplete; 315 pages including bibliographies. Outdated.

Schreiner-Yantis, Netti, ed. GENEALOGICAL & LOCAL HISTORY BOOKS
IN PRINT: A CATALOGUE. VOL. 2. Springfield, Va.: Published by the
editor, 1976.

> The same information applies to this catalog as is shown in the an-
> notation under GENEALOGICAL BOOKS IN PRINT (below). Vol-
> ume 2 is more up-to-date and serves as a companion to the pre-
> vious title.

_____. GENEALOGICAL BOOKS IN PRINT. Springfield, Va.: Published
by the editor, 1975.

> This important genealogical catalog of in-print titles gives reference
> to some articles and local records published in selected American
> genealogical periodicals. Entries are filed under the name of the
> state and thereunder by county. There are also general sections.
> Those items listed are in fact advertisements and give reference to
> where they can be purchased. Reference to the periodical title
> and volume number are shown, as well as where that item can be
> purchased. This is an excellent catalog and useful to genealogists
> and genealogical librarians. It can be obtained from the editor,
> 6818 Lois Drive, Springfield, Virginia 22150. See also the sequel,
> above.

Stanard, William Glover, comp. SOME EMIGRANTS TO VIRGINIA. 2d ed. 1915. Reprint. Baltimore: Genealogical Publishing Co., 1964.

This ninety-four page work is a personal name index to original and published records and to several genealogical periodicals. Biographical data for each person are included. Indexes several hundred colonial emigrants to Virginia. Volume and page numbers are shown.

Stewart, Robert Armistead. INDEX TO PRINTED VIRGINIA GENEALOGIES. 1930. Reprint. Baltimore: Genealogical Publishing Co., 1970.

This work is a surname index to over 700 different titles, mostly Virginia sources, published prior to 1930. Stewart includes references to over ten genealogical periodicals and a few newspapers. Approximately 6,000 surnames are represented in this index. Selective references to works published in states other than Virginia are included. Two major limitations of Stewart's INDEX are (1) it is a surname index only, and (2) there is a great deal in print since 1930 concerning Virginia families.

Swem, Earl Gregg. VIRGINIA HISTORICAL INDEX. 2 vols. in 4. Gloucester, Mass.: Peter Smith, 1965.

This monumental work indexes surnames, complete personal names, subjects, and locality records found in seven Virginia serials. The following volumes and titles are indexed:

CALENDAR OF VIRGINIA STATE PAPERS AND OTHER MANUSCRIPTS, vols. 1-11, 1875-93.

Hening's STATUTES AT LARGE, BEING A COLLECTION OF ALL THE LAWS OF VIRGINIA, 1619-1792, vols. 1-13.

THE LOWER NORFOLK COUNTY VIRGINIA ANTI-QUARY, vols. 1-5, 1895-1906.

TYLER'S QUARTERLY HISTORICAL AND GENEALOGI-CAL MAGAZINE, vols. 1-10, 1919-29.

THE VIRGINIA HISTORICAL REGISTER AND LITERARY ADVERTISER, vols. 1-6, 1848-53.

THE VIRGINIA MAGAZINE OF HISTORY AND BIOG-RAPHY, vols. 1-38, 1893-1930.

WILLIAM AND MARY COLLEGE QUARTERLY HISTORI-CAL MAGAZINE, 1st series, vols. 1-27, 1892-1919; 2d series, vols. 1-10, 1921-30.

The index references show the exact volume and page number where the item can be found in the above-listed serials. Abundant "see also" cross-references were used by Swem. This is an invaluable index for Virginia genealogists and those doing research in this area of the United States.

Wakefield, Robert S. "Index to Recent Articles on Rhode Island Families."
R.I. ROOTS 1 (Fall 1975): 1-5.

> The first section of this article serves as a surname index to three
> genealogical periodicals and one historical periodical for articles
> on Rhode Island families. Rhode Island topical articles are indexed
> in part two of this article. Not comprehensive.

WRITINGS ON AMERICAN HISTORY. 1902-- . Some years unpublished.
Current issue published by The American Historical Association, Washington,
D.C.

> An important subject bibliography to historical periodicals. In-
> cludes some genealogical periodical titles. This bibliography serves
> as a type of index to family surnames. Later volumes are separately
> indexed. The set is indexed by INDEX TO THE WRITINGS ON
> AMERICAN HISTORY, 1902-1940, for the years included.

INDEXES AT GENEALOGICAL LIBRARIES

Many libraries with genealogical collections have special indexes to their
sources, including indexes to genealogical periodicals and other printed materials. These are usually three-by-five-inch card indexes, but they are not
limited to this format. These special indexes, current or noncurrent, may index periodicals, newspapers, Bible records, and original records. Only three
of these special indexes are described in this section. Other libraries have
similar indexes. The researcher should seek out such special indexes at public
and genealogical libraries.

Old Locality File, at the Genealogical Society Library, Salt Lake City, Utah.

> This three-by-five-inch card index was formerly part of the card
> catalog at the Genealogical Society Library. Duplicate cards
> which are presently available in the library's main card catalog
> have been removed from this file, however. The Old Locality
> File is helpful in locating sources not found in the library's card
> catalog. Those cards in this file serve as subject indexes to a
> variety of original records and printed sources at the Genealogical
> Society. This index is a useful finding aid.

> Types of sources indexed include cemetery records, local histories,
> biographies, vital records, wills, Bible records, newspapers, tax
> records, church records, military records, court records, census
> records, and similar genealogical sources. Many of the sources
> included in this index are taken from genealogical periodicals.

> Various records from the United States and many foreign countries
> are included in this file. Cards are filed by localities; and, for
> the United States, they are alphabetically arranged by states,
> counties, and towns. The title of the article, subject, or source
> description is given, along with title of the publication (often ab-

breviated), volume and page numbers, and the Genealogical Society's book or microfilm number.

Personal names are not included in this file, although they would, of course, appear in the sources indexed. The Old Locality File is not kept up to date. Another limitation is that it contains obsolete library call numbers. For printed materials, the library user needs to obtain the present call number by checking in a cross-reference book available in the library's reference area.

Old Surname File, at the Genealogical Society Library, Salt Lake City.

This is a three-by-five-inch card index which is also known as the Surname Card Index, Index File, or Surname File. It is an index to some printed and original sources located at the LDS Genealogical Society Library in Salt Lake City. The index was begun ca. 1938 and was discontinued ca. 1964. It covers various time periods. Both United States and foreign sources were indexed, although it is mostly an index to United States sources. It has not been kept up to date. The index is particularly valuable for locating LDS ancestors, but it is not limited to those whose ancestors were Mormon. The Old Surname File is helpful in locating biographical sketches in books and genealogical periodicals. Other sources partially indexed include Bible records, cemetery records, local histories, and D.A.R. records.

Cards in this index are filed alphabetically by surnames. The cards show complete personal names or just surnames, for instance, "Jones Family." Many cards include a brief biographical sketch of the person, brief description of the source, and all cards show a complete or abbreviated title of the record indexed and the Genealogical Society book or microfilm number. Volume and page numbers are also shown.

This index refers the user to the printed source in the library in Salt Lake City or to the original record on microfilm where more information can be found. Copies of many of the indexed sources will be available at other libraries. Much of the information which was indexed will not be otherwise included in a composite periodicals index.

Only major personal names from selected books, periodical articles, original sources, and biographical material are included in this index. Like most composite indexes, the Old Surname File is not comprehensive. Some of the references to common family surnames are somewhat ambiguous; for example, one card reads "Smith Family --Bible Records from Ga."

The Surname File, at the Cache Genealogical Library, Logan, Utah.

This is a three-by-five-inch card index to many printed sources housed at the Cache Genealogical Library, Logan, Utah. It is similar to the Old Surname File at the Genealogical Society in Salt

Lake City (see above). Cache's Surname File indexes many genealogical periodicals received by that library. A register of those serials which are indexed has not been maintained. The index has not been kept up to date. Surnames are indexed along with complete personal names. The cards are alphabetically arranged by surname.

PERIODICAL INDEXES WHICH INCLUDE "GENEALOGY" AS A SUBJECT HEADING

When using the indexes shown in this bibliography, the researcher should look under subject headings related to genealogical research, such as "Immigration and Emigration," as well as the subject heading "Genealogy." The researcher needs to be imaginative when using these indexes. Even the subject heading "History" could yield important references. Family surnames are often indexed in a separate section in these indexes. Direct and indirect locality headings should also be checked.

The list below excludes titles of ecclesiastical periodical indexes. For example, several LDS periodical indexes include "genealogy" as a subject heading; these indexes are not listed in this bibliography.

AMERICA, HISTORY AND LIFE: A GUIDE TO PERIODICAL LITERATURE. Santa Barbara, Calif.: American Bibliographical Center, Clio Press, 1964-- .

AMERICAN HISTORY PERIODICAL INDEX. Chicago and River Grove, Ill.: Joseph A. Huebner, Russell L. Knor, 1958-67.

   Also includes family names.

ANNUAL MAGAZINE SUBJECT INDEX. See CUMULATED MAGAZINE SUBJECT INDEX, 1907-1949.

BIBLIOGRAPHIC INDEX: A CUMULATIVE BIBLIOGRAPHY OF BIBLIOGRAPHIES. New York: H.W. Wilson Co., 1937-- .

BRITISH HUMANITIES INDEX. London: Library Association, 1962-- . Current supplements.

CANADIAN INDEX TO PERIODICALS AND DOCUMENTARY FILMS. Ottawa: Canadian Library Association, 1948-- . Presently titled CANADIAN PERIODICAL INDEX.

CUMULATED MAGAZINE SUBJECT INDEX, 1907-1949. 2 vols. Boston: G.K. Hall, 1964. Formerly ANNUAL MAGAZINE SUBJECT INDEX.

CUMULATIVE INDEX TO A SELECTED LIST OF PERIODICALS. 3 vols. Edited by the Cleveland Public Library. Cleveland, Ohio: Helman-Taylor Co., 1897-99.

EDUCATION INDEX. New York: H.W. Wilson Co., 1929-- . Current supplements.

ESSAY AND GENERAL LITERATURE INDEX. New York: H.W. Wilson Co., 1900-- .

HISTORICAL ABSTRACTS. Santa Barbara, Calif.: American Bibliographical Center, 1955-- . Annual.

HUMANITIES INDEX. Edited by Elizabeth E. Pingree. New York: H.W. Wilson Co., 1976. Current supplements.

AN INDEX TO GENERAL LITERATURE (The ALA Index). 2d ed. Ann Arbor: Pierian Press, 1970.

INDEX TO PERIODICAL ARTICLES BY AND ABOUT NEGROES. Boston: G.K. Hall, 1950-72.

INDEX TO THE WRITINGS ON AMERICAN HISTORY, 1902-1940. Washington, D.C.: American Historical Association, 1956.

INTERNATIONAL INDEX TO PERIODICALS. New York: H.W. Wilson Co., 1907-65. See SOCIAL SCIENCES & HUMANITIES INDEX.

LIBRARY LITERATURE. New York: H.W. Wilson Co., 1921-- . Current supplements.

NINETEENTH CENTURY READER'S GUIDE TO PERIODICAL LITERATURE, 1890-1899; WITH SUPPLEMENTARY INDEXING, 1900-1922. 2 vols. Edited by Helen Grant Cushing and Adah. V. Morris. New York: H.W. Wilson Co., 1944.

POOLE'S INDEX TO PERIODICAL LITERATURE. Rev. ed. 2 vols. Boston: Houghton, 1891. Originally edited by William Frederick Poole, vol. 1, 1802-81; supplements, 5 vols., 1882-1906. See also CUMULATIVE AUTHOR INDEX FOR QUERY POOL'S INDEX TO PERIODICAL LITERATURE, 1802-1906, compiled and edited by C. Edward Wall, Ann Arbor: Pierian Press, 1971.

POPULAR PERIODICAL INDEX. Edited by Robert M. Bottorff. Camden, N.J., 1974-- . Semiannual.

READER'S GUIDE TO PERIODICAL LITERATURE. New York: H.W. Wilson Co., 1905-- . Cumulated from 1900. Current supplements.

SOCIAL SCIENCES & HUMANITIES INDEX. New York: H.W. Wilson Co., 1916-- . Formerly titled INTERNATIONAL INDEX. Current supplements.

THE SUBJECT INDEX TO PERIODICALS. London: Library Association, 1919-62.

Appendix 2

BIBLIOGRAPHICAL CONTROL

Genealogy has undergone an information explosion during the twentieth century. The volume, variety, and location of genealogical writings has multiplied drastically during the 1960s and 1970s, making bibliographical control increasingly difficult.[1] Genealogical and historical writings are increasing rapidly; the literature continues to grow enormously and steadily. These writings can be found in well-known, formal publications, as well as smaller, isolated periodicals. Each serial makes its own unique contribution to the field of genealogy.

The demand on genealogical research sources is constantly increasing. As interest in genealogical and historical research is propagated, the problem of bibliographical control of periodical literature becomes more complex. This is a dilemma for the genealogist since a major portion of genealogical research activity is dependent upon genealogical periodicals.

Some genealogical periodicals, particularly family magazines, publish only a limited number of issues; this sometimes makes the publication difficult for the researcher to identify, and copies difficult to locate. It is often a challenge for the genealogist to obtain copies of needed serials. The researcher therefore needs to rely on the available bibliographic tools.

The purpose of this appendix is to list and describe sources which contain bibliographical information concerning American genealogical periodical literature. Two of the references cited, NEW SERIAL TITLES: A UNION LIST OF SERIALS COMMENCING PUBLICATION AFTER DECEMBER 31, 1949 and UNION LIST OF SERIALS IN LIBRARIES OF THE UNITED STATES AND CANADA, show the location of some genealogical serials by titles in major libraries throughout the country, as well as other helpful bibliographical information. These two union lists are incomplete, however.

Omitted from this appendix are serials lists of libraries housing genealogical periodicals. As an example, both the Genealogical Society Library in Salt Lake City and the Harold B. Lee Library at Brigham Young University, Provo, Utah, house a number of genealogical serials and both have formal serials lists describing their serials holdings, as do other libraries.

A pioneer bibliography of genealogical periodicals was compiled by Lester J. Cappon in 1964, entitled AMERICAN GENEALOGICAL PERIODICALS: A BIBLIOGRAPHY WITH A CHRONOLOGICAL FINDING-LIST. This is one of the most extensive bibliographies of genealogical periodicals. As Cappon discovered in preparing this bibliography, a major problem in identifying genealogical periodicals is that many are ephemeral.

American Association for State and Local History. DIRECTORY, HISTORICAL SOCIETIES AND AGENCIES IN THE UNITED STATES AND CANADA. Nashville: American Association for State and Local History. Biennial. 10th edition compiled and edited by Donna McDonald, 1975.

> An extensive listing of historical societies in the United States and Canada. Includes names of many genealogical societies. Serial titles are sometimes included in the entries. Also shown are addresses, year founded, number of members, and other information. Contains several indexes to names of societies. This is an important reference work for American genealogists and historians.

Arndt, Karl J.R., and Olson, May E., comps. GERMAN-AMERICAN NEWSPAPERS AND PERIODICALS, 1732-1955: HISTORY AND BIBLIOGRAPHY. 2d rev. ed. New York: Johnson Reprint, 1965. Volume 2 entitled THE GERMAN LANGUAGE PRESS OF THE AMERICAS, 1732-1968: HISTORY AND BIBLIOGRAPHY. Pullach/Munchen: Verlag Dokumentation, 1973.

> Although not genealogically oriented, this work is included here for its historical significance, especially for the German-American genealogist. Includes references to German periodical titles. Another important bibliography is by Carl Frederick Wittke, THE GERMAN-LANGUAGE PRESS IN AMERICA (New York: Haskell House Publishers, 1973). This latter work includes bibliographical references for this topic and is another important source for German-American newspaper titles.

AYER DIRECTORY OF PUBLICATIONS. Philadelphia: Ayer Press, 1869-- . Annual.

> Although this lists mostly information about newspapers, some periodical titles are given, including genealogical periodicals. Arranged by localities in the United States and Canada, then by title. Entries show year established, frequency of publication, address, and other data. This is an incomplete listing of genealogical serials. Indexed.

Bierman, Edwinna, comp. DIRECTORY, GENEALOGICAL SOCIETIES AND PERIODICALS IN THE UNITED STATES. San Gabriel, Calif.: Edwinna Bierman, 1965.

> An outdated directory of genealogical societies in the United States. Annotated entries show titles of serials published by these societies. The information given about cost and addresses is usually now ob-

solete. This work also includes a section of "how to" articles, including types and uses of genealogical queries. Two other sections will be of interest to American genealogists: "Genealogical Columns in Newspapers," and "Genealogical Periodicals Devoted Solely to Queries."

Boehm, Eric H., and Adolphus, Lalit, eds. HISTORICAL PERIODICALS: AN ANNOTATED WORLD LIST OF HISTORICAL AND RELATED SERIAL PUBLICATIONS. Santa Barbara, Calif.: Clio Press, 1961.

An international listing of serial titles. Some genealogical serial titles are included. Shows cost and addresses, although that information is out of date. Indexed.

Brown, Erma Lee Skyles, comp. 1975 UNITED STATES GENEALOGICAL SOCIETIES AND PUBLICATIONS LISTING. Salem, Oregon: privately published, 1975. 15 p.

Although the format is not of high quality, this is a fair listing of United States genealogical periodicals. Arranged by state, name of the organization, and title of serial. Shows addresses.

Cappon, Lester J. AMERICAN GENEALOGICAL PERIODICALS: A BIBLIOGRAPHY WITH A CHRONOLOGICAL FINDING-LIST. New York: New York Public Library, 1964.

Although outdated, this is one of the most extensive bibliographies of United States genealogical periodicals yet compiled. Entries are alphabetically arranged by title and show publication dates, by whom published, name of editor(s), size of serial, and other information. Retrospective titles are also shown. The compiler has included two other sections: "Chronological Finding-List by Date of Establishment," and "Geographical Finding-List by State."

Filby, P. William, comp. AMERICAN & BRITISH GENEALOGY & HERALDRY: A SELECTED LIST OF BOOKS. 2d ed. Chicago: American Library Association, 1975.

This scholarly genealogical reference book includes titles of genealogical serials under various headings and localities. The title of the serial is shown along with the beginning year, place published, and publisher. Most entries are annotated. Each entry listed in this work is assigned its own unique number. Well indexed.

GENEALOGICAL PERIODICAL ANNUAL INDEX, Vols. 1-4, 1962-65. Edited by Ellen Stanley Rogers. Bladensburg, Md.: Genealogical Recorders, 1963-67. Vols. 5-8, 1966-69. Compiled and published by George Ely Russell. Mitchellville, Md., 1967-73. Vols. 13 and 14, 1974-75. Edited by Laird C. Towle. Bowie, Md., 1976-77. 1970-73 unpublished.

See chapter 7, above.

Heiss, Willard. "Serendipity." GENEALOGY, no. 10, November 1974, pp. 17-20.

> A three-page listing of titles of family periodicals. Shows addresses and cost of each periodical. An incomplete list.

Helmbold, F. Wilbur. TRACING YOUR ANCESTRY: A STEP-BY-STEP GUIDE TO RESEARCHING YOUR FAMILY HISTORY. Birmingham, Ala.: Oxmoor House, 1976.

> On pages 198-205 in the bibliography to this beginning text is a listing of United States genealogical periodicals. A general section is followed by each state alphabetically arranged by title. Only a few serial titles are given for each state. Addresses of each publication are shown. This bibliography is incomplete, however.

THE HEREDITARY REGISTER OF THE UNITED STATES OF AMERICA. Washington, D.C.: United States Hereditary Register, 1972-- . Annual.

> This publication includes a listing of family associations in the United States. Titles of family serials are included, along with addresses. This is a good list of family organizations and titles of family magazines. The researcher should use the most current edition.

IRREGULAR SERIALS & ANNUALS: AN INTERNATIONAL DIRECTORY. New York: R.R. Bowker, 1967-- . Biennial.

> Genealogical serial titles which are published irregularly are listed under the heading "Genealogy and Heraldry." Cost and addresses are shown. International in scope. The researcher should also see the titles under the heading "History." This work includes a listing of discontinued serial titles.

Jacobus, Donald Lines. INDEX TO GENEALOGICAL PERIODICALS. 3 vols. 1932, 1948, 1953. Reprint (3 vols. in 1). Baltimore: Genealogical Publishing Co., 1963, 1973.

> See chapter 5, above.

Kaminkow, Marion J., ed. GENEALOGIES IN THE LIBRARY OF CONGRESS: A BIBLIOGRAPHY. 3 vols. Baltimore: Magna Carta Book Co., 1972, 1977.

> This important reference work lists titles of about 250 family magazines, many of which were published before ca. 1940. Shows title of serial and publishing dates. This three-volume work is an excellent bibliography of many published, and some manuscript, family histories in the Library of Congress, Washington, D.C. Genealogists should use this bibliography to determine the existence of family histories in the Library of Congress.

The 1977 supplement is entitled GENEALOGIES IN THE LIBRARY
OF CONGRESS: A BIBLIOGRAPHY, SUPPLEMENT, 1972-1976.
LIBRARY JOURNAL has called this "the most comprehensive bib-
liography of family histories of America and Great Britain avail-
able." The supplement lists books added to the collections of the
Library of Congress from 1972 to July 1976.

Katz, Bill [William Armstrong], and Gargal, Berry. MAGAZINES FOR LI-
BRARIES. 2d ed. New York: R.R. Bowker, 1972. SECOND EDITION
SUPPLEMENT. New York: R.R. Bowker, 1974.

Includes a section entitled "Genealogy and Heraldry." Entries are
annotated; shows cost and addresses. The genealogist should also
refer to the serials under the heading "History." Shows reference
to indexing services for some titles. Not comprehensive.

Konrad, J. A DIRECTORY OF GENEALOGICAL PERIODICALS. Munroe Falls,
Ohio: Summit Publications, 1975.

This sixty-one page booklet is divided into five sections:

1. Periodicals Published by Societies in the United States
2. Periodicals Published by Firms and Individuals in the
   United States
3. Periodicals Published Outside of the United States
4. Family "One Name" Newsletters, Published in the United States
5. Family One Name Newsletters Published in Europe

There is an addenda and the work is unindexed. The frequency of
publication is shown for each serial along with the cost and address.

McCay, Betty L., comp. FAMILY SURNAME PUBLICATIONS. Indianapolis:
Ye Olde Genealogie Shoppe, 1975.

This eighteen-page booklet is an alphabetical listing of over 250
family newsletters, bulletins, and quarterlies. The following information is shown for each entry: title of the serial, by whom published, address of publisher, and frequency and cost of the serial.
Some entries indicate if queries are accepted for publication, and
an indication of any available indexes to the serial is sometimes
shown. Dates of publication (beginning and ending dates) of the
serials are not shown. Surname cross-references are included. This
booklet will be helpful in finding data concerning many of the
family magazines which have been published in the United States.
As can be expected, some of the addresses and cost of each publication are outdated.

Meyer, Mary Keysor, ed. DIRECTORY OF GENEALOGICAL SOCIETIES IN THE
U.S.A. AND CANADA WITH AN APPENDED LIST OF INDEPENDENT GENEA-
LOGICAL PERIODICALS. Pasadena, Md.: Published by the editor, 1976.

This seventy-three page booklet lists names of many genealogical societies in the United States and Canada. Many entries show the title of their serial or special publication(s). A number of entries state "Registration not Received." The editor lists a serial title only if her questionnaire was returned. A seven-page appendix is entitled, "The Independent Genealogical Periodicals," which lists serials not associated with a formal organization. The work is well indexed, except for serial titles which are not indexed.

Section I of this booklet is a directory of genealogical societies, arranged by Canadian province, then alphabetically by each state of the United States, and thereunder alphabetically by city. Some of the bibliographic information is outdated, some incomplete, some incorrect. A number of important genealogical serial titles are not included in this DIRECTORY. Titles of family magazines are also omitted, although these are often helpful in American genealogical research. It would be helpful to have a listing of family and surname periodicals.

In spite of these limitations, this is an important listing of American genealogical societies and serial titles. All libraries in North America with a genealogical collection should have this reference source. A revised directory is scheduled for publication in 1978. This DIRECTORY is available from Mrs. Mary K. Meyer, 297 Cove Road, Pasadena, Maryland 21122.

Mid-Michigan Genealogical Society. A BRIEF GUIDE TO AMERICAN GENEA-LOGICAL SOCIETIES AND PERIODICALS. Occasional Paper, no. 6. Lansing: 1975.

A forty-five page booklet which lists titles of genealogical serials and genealogical societies under three headings: (1) general, (2) alphabetical by state, and (3) general interest. Only United States serial titles are shown, along with the cost and frequency of publication. Indexed. Outdated.

Miller, Olga K. MIGRATION, EMIGRATION, IMMIGRATION: PRINCIPALLY TO THE UNITED STATES AND IN THE UNITED STATES. Logan, Utah: Everton Publishers, 1974.

An important bibliography which lists 290 American and foreign serial titles in the appendix to this work. For many of the serial titles in the appendix, the address is shown; this adds to the usefulness of this bibliography. Some Genealogical Society Library call numbers are given.

NEW SERIAL TITLES: A UNION LIST OF SERIALS COMMENCING PUBLICA-TION AFTER DECEMBER 31, 1949. Washington, D.C.: Library of Congress, 1953-- .

Updates UNION LIST OF SERIALS (see below), published by the H.W. Wilson Company. NEW SERIAL TITLES is kept current by

supplements. It has a two-volume subject guide, 1950-70, and a
four-volume 1950-1970 CUMULATIVE (New York: R.R. Bowker,
1973). This set is the most comprehensive of the bibliographies
and union lists of serial titles. Includes genealogical and historical periodical titles. Known library holdings are shown for serial
titles. Serial titles are alphabetically arranged. A search of this
union list is essential for identifying the location of periodical
titles; genealogists should therefore familiarize themselves with
this union list.

New York (City). Public Library. Local History and Genealogy Division.
DICTIONARY CATALOG OF THE LOCAL HISTORY AND GENEALOGY DIVI-
SION. 18 vols. Boston: G.K. Hall, 1974.

This extensive catalog lists genealogical and historical serial titles
alphabetically by title, along with titles of other sources. Shows
dates and volume numbers of serials held by the New York Public
Library, New York City. Cataloger's notes serve as brief annotations. This is an important reference source. Researchers should
take advantage of the vast genealogical holdings at the New York
Public Library.

Pitoni, Ven, comp. GUIDEX, GENEALOGICAL RESEARCH GUIDE TO PRIN-
CIPAL SOURCES AND INDEXES. Annapolis, Md.: Family Guidex, 1946.

Lists some genealogical periodical titles. Not comprehensive.
Outdated.

St. Louis Genealogical Society. TOPICAL INDEX OF GENEALOGICAL
QUARTERLIES. Compiled by Geraldine Bailey, St. Louis: 1973-- .

See chapter 8, above.

Schreiner-Yantis, Netti, ed. GENEALOGICAL & LOCAL HISTORY BOOKS IN
PRINT: A CATALOGUE. Vol. 2. Springfield, Va.: Published by the editor,
1976.

Volume 2 of this paperback catalog lists titles of family magazines
and newsletters in a section entitled "Family Genealogies." Shows
bibliographic information including reference to where that serial
can be purchased. This section of the catalog is indexed by surnames, similar to GENEALOGICAL BOOKS IN PRINT by the same
editor (see below). Titles of many other genealogical periodicals
are also shown throughout this important reference book. Genealogical libraries will need this work as a companion to GENEA-
LOGICAL BOOKS IN PRINT.

_____. GENEALOGICAL BOOKS IN PRINT. Springfield, Va.: Published
by the editor, 1975.

Lists titles of family magazines and newsletters in a section entitled

"Family Genealogies & Newsletters." An excellent list of titles.
Shows bibliographic information including cost and reference to
where that serial can be purchased. This section of the catalog
is indexed by surnames. Titles of many other genealogical periodicals are also shown under the name of each respective state.

A useful catalog of in-print genealogical and historical titles.
This catalog is a "must" for genealogical libraries. A great number
of otherwise hidden genealogical sources have been amassed in this
economically priced catalog. This is an important acquisitions
source for the genealogical librarian. The catalog is available
from the editor at 6818 Lois Drive, Springfield, Virginia 22150.
See sequel, above.

Severance, Henry Ormal, comp. A GUIDE TO THE CURRENT PERIODICALS
AND SERIALS OF THE UNITED STATES AND CANADA. 4th ed. Ann Arbor:
George Wahr, 1920.

Lists titles of a few genealogical periodicals. Indexed. Outdated.

.THE STANDARD PERIODICAL DIRECTORY. Edited by Leon Garry. New York:
Oxbridge Publishing Co., 1964/65-- . Annual.

The 1973 (4th) edition lists ninety serial titles under the heading
"Genealogy" (071). Brief descriptive annotations are given, as
well as cost and addresses. Includes reference to genealogical
periodicals, family publications, and GENEALOGICAL PERIODI-
CAL ANNUAL INDEX. Shows United States and Canadian serial
titles. Includes titles of three heraldic serials published in London.
Incomplete; partially outdated. The genealogist should also refer
to the "History" section (084) for historical periodical titles; this
section is more extensive than the genealogy section.

Townsend, Mrs. Charles D., and Jacobus, Donald Lines. "Current Genealogical Periodicals." THE AMERICAN GENEALOGIST 38 (1962): 116-28. Supplement in THE AMERICAN GENEALOGIST 39 (1963): 61-64.

This article and supplement list some of the major genealogical
periodicals published in the United States. Annotated. Some of
the information is now outdated. An incomplete list.

ULRICH'S INTERNATIONAL PERIODICALS DIRECTORY. New York: R.R.
Bowker Co., 1932-- . Annual.

Lists many genealogical titles under the heading "Genealogy and
Heraldry." Includes cost and addresses. Not comprehensive but
is reasonably current. Interested genealogists should also see the
serial titles under the heading "History." International in scope.
Researchers should use the current edition.

UNION LIST OF SERIALS IN LIBRARIES OF THE UNITED STATES AND CANA-
DA. 5 vols. 3d ed. Edited by Edna Brown Titus. New York: H.W. Wilson
Co., 1965.

An alphabetical listing of serial titles including genealogical periodicals. Shows publication information and some libraries which
house the serial. This union list is not complete with regard to
holdings of libraries. Updated by NEW SERIAL TITLES (see above).

NOTES

1. One definition of bibliographical control has been given as "the devices and
services which enable any investigator to discover, locate and obtain whatever
segment of man's record of his thinking activities, experiences and knowledge
he may want, for whatever purpose . . . be it a single thought, an elusive
fact, a new idea, or the most comprehensive chronicle of an extinct civiliza-
tion," Mrs. Kathrine Oliver Murra, "UNESCO/Library of Congress Bibliographical Survey: First Interim Report of the Library of Congress Bibliographical
Planning Group, June 1949," COLLEGE AND RESEARCH LIBRARIES 10 (1949):
407-8; see also Jacqueline Page Bull, "Bibliographical Control of State Historical Material," SOUTHEASTERN LIBRARIAN 5 (1955): 49.

Appendix 3

AMERICAN GENEALOGICAL PERIODICALS:

A SELECT LIST

This appendix contains a selected list of titles of genealogical periodicals published in the United States and Canada. A few historical and specialized serial titles are also included. The serials listed here publish articles and other material of interest to American genealogists. This material might include genealogies and pedigrees, abstracts from records, descriptions of genealogical sources, genealogical queries, book reviews, and news notes. Most of these items are of lasting reference value.

Within this criterion, many retrospective and discontinued serial titles are included, since these have material of interest to genealogists. Retrospective serials may be indexed in the composite indexes mentioned earlier in this book. Other serial titles are listed because of their contributions to American genealogy. Cross-references have been used, referring the reader from a discontinued title to the current title.

Ephemeral titles and those with low circulation are generally excluded from this bibliography. Also omitted are titles of periodicals, newsletters, and bulletins of family associations and family organizations. Most newsletters and bulletins of genealogical organizations have been omitted, since these publications are too numerous to mention here. However, those newsletters which are included offer notable contributions to American genealogy. Also excluded from this list are historical serials which publish only articles of a historical nature with little or no genealogical information.

Titles are arranged alphabetically, followed by the name of the publisher and address where that periodical can be obtained. Cost of each serial has been omitted because the prices change so frequently. This appendix should, however, be useful as an acquisitions list for genealogists and genealogical librarians.

The first column following the title and address indicates the general scope of the serial. In analyzing the periodicals, the scope of some of them was difficult to ascertain because the contents of issues varied. The following legend has been used in determining scope:

Select List of Periodicals

E - ethnic	N - national
I - international	R - regional
L - local	S - specialized

The second column shows the frequency of publication. This may have varied among issues of the same title. When appropriate, numeric designations have been used to show the number of issues published annually. The following legend is used to show frequency of publication:

A - annual	Q - quarterly
B - bimonthly	SA - semiannual
IR - irregular	W - weekly
M - monthly	

A single asterisk (*) in the third column indicates those titles which should be in all libraries housing genealogical materials in North America, regardless of size (in the opinion of the author). Genealogists and genealogical librarians should be especially familiar with the contents of those titles marked with a single asterisk.

A double asterisk (**) in the third column indicates those serials which should be in the collections of medium size libraries—in addition to those titles marked with a single asterisk. Larger libraries housing genealogical materials will want to subscribe to most of the current serial titles shown in this list. Libraries will want to subscribe to those titles published in their own state, and possibly neighboring states or that region.

TITLE OF PERIODICAL, ADDRESS	SCOPE	FREQUENCY OF PUBLICATION	PRIORITY
ACADIAN GENEALOGY EXCHANGE. Mrs. Janet Jehn, ed., 863 Wayman Branch Road, Covington, KY 41015	S	Q	**
THE ALABAMA GENEALOGICAL REGISTER. 1959-68. Elizabeth Wood Thomas, ed., Pass Christian, MS	L	Q	
ALABAMA GENEALOGICAL SOCIETY, INC., MAGAZINE. 2 Brantwood Drive, Montgomery, AL 36109	L	Q	
THE AMERICAN ARCHIVIST. Society of American Archivists, 801 South Morgan, Chicago, IL 60680	N	Q	**

TITLE OF PERIODICAL, ADDRESS	SCOPE	FREQUENCY OF PUBLICATION	PRIORITY
AMERICAN COLLEGE OF HERALDRY JOURNAL. American College of Heraldry, Box 5007, New Orleans, LA 70118	S	B	
THE AMERICAN GENEALOGIST. George E. McCracken, ed., 1232 39th Street, Des Moines, IA 50311	N	Q	*
AMERICAN HERITAGE SERVICE. Mrs. Shirley Foradori and Mrs. V. Loretta Wolfe, Austin, TX (disc.)	N	Q	
AMERICAN HISTORICAL SOCIETY OF GERMANS FROM RUSSIA: WORK PAPERS. 631 D Street, Lincoln, NE 68502	S/E	IR	
AMERICAN JEWISH ARCHIVES. Hebrew Union College, Cincinnati, OH 45220	E	SA	
THE AMERICAN JOURNAL OF LEGAL HISTORY. Temple University School of Law, 1715 North Broad Street, Philadelphia, PA 19122	S	Q	
THE AMERICAN MONTHLY MAGAZINE. See DAUGHTERS OF THE AMERICAN REVOLUTION MAGAZINE			
THE AMERICAN REGISTER. 1926-32. Shawver Publishing Co., Morrison, IL	N	M	
AMERICANA. 1906-43. (Originally AMERICAN HISTORICAL MAGAZINE). American Historical Co., Inc., New York, NY	N	Q	
ANCESTOR HUNT. Ashtabula County Genealogical Society, c/o Henderson Library, 54 East Jefferson Street, Jefferson, OH 44047	L	Q	

Select List of Periodicals

TITLE OF PERIODICAL, ADDRESS	SCOPE	FREQUENCY OF PUBLICATION	PRIORITY
ANCESTORS WEST. Santa Barbara County Genealogical Society, P.O. Box 1174, Goleta, CA 93017	L	Q	
ANCESTRAL NEWS. Ancestral Trails Historical Society, P.O. Box 573, Vine Grove, KY 40175	L	Q	
ANCESTRAL NOTES FROM CHED-WATO. 1954-68. Chedwato Service, Burlington, VT	N	B	
ANCESTRY. Palm Beach County Genealogical Society, P.O. Box 1746, West Palm Beach, FL 33402	L	Q	
ANNALS OF IOWA. Iowa State Historical Department, East 12th and Grand Avenue, Des Moines, IA 50319	L	Q	
"ANSEARCHIN'" NEWS. Tennessee Genealogical Society, P.O. Box 12124, Memphis, TN 38112	L	Q	
THE APPLELAND BULLETIN. Genea-logical Society of North Central Washington, P.O. Box 613, Wenat-chee, WA 98801	L	Q	
AREA KEYS GENEALOGICAL MAGAZINE. Florence Clint, ed., P.O. Box 19465, Denver, CO 80219	S	IR	
THE ARKANSAS FAMILY HISTORIAN. Arkansas Genealogical Society, Inc., 4200 A Street, Little Rock, AR 72205	L	Q	
THE ARKANSAS GENEALOGICAL REGISTER. Northeast Arkansas Gene-alogical Association, 314 Vine Street, Newport, AR 72112	L	Q	

TITLE OF PERIODICAL, ADDRESS	SCOPE	FREQUENCY OF PUBLICATION	PRIORITY
ARKANSAS GENEALOGICAL RE-SEARCH AID. Counts Genealogical Research & Publications, North Little Rock, AR	L	Q	
THE ARKANSAS RESEARCHER. 1962-64. Allstates Research Co., Murray, UT	L	A	
ASH TREE ECHO. Fresno Genea-logical Society, P.O. Box 2042, Fresno, CA 93718	L	Q	
ATHELINGS. 710 Flora Vista Drive, Santa Barbara, CA 93109	L	Q	
THE AUGUSTAN. 1510 Cravens Avenue, Torrance, CA 90501	S	Q	**
AUSTIN GENEALOGICAL SOCIETY QUARTERLY. P.O. Box 774, Austin, TX 78767	L	Q	
THE BACKTRACKER. Northwest Arkansas Genealogical Society, P.O. Box 362, Rogers, AR 72756	L	Q	
BACKTRACKING. Olympic Gene-alogical Society, Route 5, Box 747F, Bremerton, WA 98310	L	Q	
THE BANGOR HISTORICAL MAGA-ZINE. See THE MAIN HISTORICAL MAGAZINE			
BEAVER BRIEFS. Willamette Valley Genealogical Society. P.O. Box 2083, Salem, OR 97308	L	Q	
THE BENTON COUNTY PIONEER. Benton County Historical Society, P.O. Box 355, Siloam Springs, AR 72761	L	Q	

TITLE OF PERIODICAL, ADDRESS	SCOPE	FREQUENCY OF PUBLICATION	PRIORITY
BISMARCK-MANDAN HISTORICAL AND GENEALOGICAL SOCIETY QUARTERLY. P.O. Box 485, Bismarck, ND 58501	L	IR	
BITS AND PIECES. Box 746, Newcastle, WY 82701	L	Q	
BLACK HILLS NUGGETS. Rapid City Society for Genealogical Research Inc., P.O. Box 1495, Rapid City, SD 57709	L	Q	
BLUE MOUNTAIN HERITAGE. Walla Walla Valley Genealogical Society, P.O. Box 115, Walla Walla, WA 99362	L	Q	
BOULDER GENEALOGICAL SOCIETY QUARTERLY. P.O. Box 3246, Boulder, CO 80303	L	Q	
BRANCHES & TWIGS. Genealogical Society of Vermont, Westminster West, RFD 3, Putney, VT 05346	L	Q	
BRANCHING OUT FROM ST. CLAIR COUNTY, ILLINOIS. Marissa Historical & Genealogical Society, P.O. Box 27, Marissa, IL 62257	L	Q	
BRIDGE BUILDER. National Pontius Society, 1787 West 5300 South, Roy, UT 84007	L	SA	
THE BRITISH COLUMBIA GENEALOGIST. P.O. Box 94371, Richmond, British Columbia V6Y 2A8	L	Q	
THE BULLETIN. See THE ONTARIO GENEALOGICAL SOCIETY BULLETIN; superseded by FAMILIES			

TITLE OF PERIODICAL, ADDRESS	SCOPE	FREQUENCY OF PUBLICATION	PRIORITY
BULLETIN, GENEALOGICAL FORUM OF PORTLAND, OREGON, INC. See GENEALOGICAL FORUM OF PORTLAND, OREGON, INC., BULLETIN			
BULLETIN OF THE OKLAHOMA GENEALOGICAL SOCIETY. See OKLAHOMA GENEALOGICAL SOCIETY QUARTERLY			
BULLETIN OF THE STAMFORD GENEALOGICAL SOCIETY. See CONNECTICUT ANCESTRY			
BULLETIN OF THE WHATCOM GENEALOGICAL SOCIETY. See WHATCOM GENEALOGICAL SOCIETY BULLETIN			
CALIFORNIA CENTRAL COAST GENEALOGICAL SOCIETY BULLETIN. P.O. BOX 832, Morro Bay, CA 93442	N	Q	
CANADIAN-AMERICAN QUERY EXCHANGE. See LOST IN CANADA?			
THE CANADIAN HISTORICAL REVIEW. Canadian Historical Association, Public Archives, Ottawa, Canada K1A 0N3	N	Q	
THE CAPE MAY COUNTY MAGAZINE OF HISTORY AND GENEALOGY. Cape May Court House, NJ 08210	L	A	
CAR-DEL SCRIBE. Charles and Edna Townsend, RFD 3, Box 120-A, Middleboro, MA C2346	S	6/yr	**

Select List of Periodicals

TITLE OF PERIODICAL, ADDRESS	SCOPE	FREQUENCY OF PUBLICATION	PRIORITY
THE CAROLINA GENEALOGIST. Heritage Papers, Route 2, Box 86, Danielsville, GA 30633	L	Q	
THE CAROLINA HERALD. South Carolina Genealogical Society, P.O. Box 11353, Columbia, SC 29211	L	Q	
THE CARROLL COUNTY HISTORICAL SOCIETY QUARTERLY. P.O. Box 249, Berryville, AR 72616	L	Q	
CENTRAL CALIFORNIA GENEALOGICAL SOCIETY, INC. P.O. Box 832, Morro Bay, CA 93442	L	Q	
CENTRAL ILLINOIS GENEALOGICAL QUARTERLY. Decatur Genealogical Society, P.O. Box 2068, Decatur, IL 62526	L	Q	
CENTRAL KENTUCKY RESEARCHER. Taylor County Historical Society, P.O. Box 14, Campbellsville, KY 42718	L	M	
CENTRAL TEXAS GENEALOGICAL SOCIETY. QUARTERLY. See HEART OF TEXAS RECORDS			
CENTRE COUNTY HERITAGE. Box 629, Bellefonte, PA 16823	L	SA	
THE CERTIFIED COPY. Greater Cleveland Genealogical Society, P.O. Box 9639, Cleveland, OH 44140	L	M	
CHAMBLESS QUARTERLY. Herring Genealogical Enterprises, Box 232, Morrow, GA 30260	L	Q	

TITLE OF PERIODICAL, ADDRESS	SCOPE	FREQUENCY OF PUBLICATION	PRIORITY
CHEROKEE COUNTY HERITAGE. P.O. Box 57, Cedar Bluff, AL 35959	L	Q	
CHICAGO GENEALOGIST. Chicago Genealogical Society, P.O. Box 1160, Chicago, IL 60690	L	Q	
CHIPS AND SHIPS. Bay County Genealogical Society, P.O. Box 27, Essexville, MI 48732	L	Q	
CHIVALRY. Hartwell Co. 1510 Cravens Avenue, Torrance, CA 90501	S	5/yr	
CHRONICLES OF ST. MARY'S. St. Mary's County, Maryland Historical Society, Abell, MD 20606	L	M	
THE CIRCUIT RIDER. Sangamon County Genealogical Society, P.O. Box 1829, Springfield, IL 62705	L	Q	
CLUES. American Historical Society of Germans from Russia, 615 D Street, Lincoln, NE 68502	S	A	
COLONIAL COURIER. Daughters of American Colonists, 2250 South Arlington Avenue, Reno, NV 89502	L	Q	
THE COLONIAL GENEALOGIST (earlier issues published in THE AUGUSTAN). Hartwell Co., 1510 Cravens Avenue, Torrance, CA 90501	S/R	IR	**
THE COLORADO GENEALOGIST. Colorado Genealogical Society, P.O. Box 9671, Denver, CO 80209	L	Q	

TITLE OF PERIODICAL, ADDRESS	SCOPE	FREQUENCY OF PUBLICATION	PRIORITY
CONNECTICUT ANCESTRY. (Formerly BULLETIN OF THE STAMFORD GENEALOGICAL SOCIETY) Stamford Genealogical Society, Inc., P.O. Box 249, Stamford, CT 06904	L	Q	**
THE CONNECTICUT MAGAZINE (formerly THE CONNECTICUT QUARTERLY). 1895-1908. Connecticut Magazine Co., Hartford and New Haven, CT	L	Q	
THE CONNECTICUT NUTMEGGER (formerly THE NUTMEGGER). Connecticut Society of Genealogists, Inc., P.O. Box 435, Glastonbury, CT 06033	L	Q	**
THE CONNECTICUT QUARTERLY. See THE CONNECTICUT MAGAZINE			
COOS GENEALOGICAL FORUM BULLETIN. P.O. Box 1067, North Bend, OR 97459	L	Q	
COPPER STATE BULLETIN (formerly SOUTHERN ARIZONA GENEALOGICAL SOCIETY BULLETIN). Arizona State Genealogical Society, P.O. Box 6027, Tucson, AZ 85733	L	Q	
CORNERSTONE CLUES. Cornerstone Genealogical Society, P.O. Box 547, Waynesburg, PA 15370	L	Q	
CORNSILKS. Genealogical Society of DeKalb County, Illinois, P.O. Box 295, Sycamore, IL 60178	L	Q	
COUSIN HUNTIN' (query publication). Central New York Genealogical Society, Box 104, Colvin Station, Syracuse, NY 13205	L	Q	

TITLE OF PERIODICAL, ADDRESS	SCOPE	FREQUENCY OF PUBLICATION	PRIORITY
COWETA CHATTER. Coweta Chatter Genealogical and Historical Society, Highway 54, Route 1, Sharpsburg, GA 30277	L	Q	
COWLITZ COUNTY HISTORICAL QUARTERLY. Courthouse Annex, Kelso, WA 98626	L	Q	
CUESTIONES: SPANISH AMERICAN GENEALOGICAL QUERIES. Hartwell Co., 1510 Cravens Avenue, Torrance, CA 90501	S	IR	
CUMBERLAND AND COLES COUNTIES GENEALOGICAL QUARTERLY. R.R. 1, Box 141, Toledo, IL 62468	L	Q	
DAKOTA TERRITORY. Black Hills Genealogy Club, P.O. Box 372, Rapid City, SD 57701	L	Q	
DAUGHTERS OF THE AMERICAN REVOLUTION MAGAZINE (formerly THE AMERICAN MONTHLY MAGAZINE). National Society, Daughters of the American Revolution, 1776 D Street, N.W., Washington, DC 20006	S/N	10/yr	**
DAY TO REMEMBER. Mrs. M.Y. Aday, Box 15468, Lakewood, CO 80215	L	Q	
DEAR GENIE. Linn County Heritage Society, Inc., P.O. Box 175, Cedar Rapids, IA 52406	L	Q	
DEEP SOUTH GENEALOGICAL QUARTERLY. Mobile Genealogical Society, Inc., P.O. Box 6224, Mobile, AL 36606	R	Q	**

TITLE OF PERIODICAL, ADDRESS	SCOPE	FREQUENCY OF PUBLICATION	PRIORITY
DE HALVE MAEN. Holland Society of New York, 122 East 58th Street, New York, NY 10022	L/S	Q	
DEKALB COUNTY HERITAGE. DeKalb County Historical Society, Route 3, Box 100, Maysville, MO 64469	L	Q	
THE DESCENDER. Montgomery County Genealogical Society, Box 444, Coffeyville, KS 67337	L	Q	
THE DES MOINES COUNTY GENE-ALOGICAL QUARTERLY. P.O. Box 493, Burlington, IA 52601	L	Q	
THE DETROIT SOCIETY FOR GENE-ALOGICAL RESEARCH MAGAZINE. 5201 Woodward Avenue, Detroit, MI 48202	R	Q	*
DE WITT COUNTY GENEALOGICAL QUARTERLY. P.O. Box 329, Clinton, IL 61727	L	Q	
DIABLO DESCENDANTS NEWS-LETTER. Contra Costa County Gene-alogical Society, P.O. Box 910, Concord, CA 94522	L	Q	
DIGGER'S DIGEST. Sutter-Yuba Genealogical Society, P.O. Box 1274, Yuba City, CA 95991	L	Q	
DOTHAN DISTRICT GENEALOGICAL EXCHANGE. 13 Bird Circle, Ozark, AL 36360	L	Q	
DUSTY TRAILS. Sybil Cornett Barker, Patty Webb Eubanks, eds., 3813 Cashion Place, Oklahoma City, OK 73112	L	Q	

TITLE OF PERIODICAL, ADDRESS	SCOPE	FREQUENCY OF PUBLICATION	PRIORITY
THE DUTCHESS. Dutchess County Genealogical Society, P.O. Box 708, Poughkeepsie, NY 12602	L	Q	
DUTCHESS COUNTY HISTORICAL SOCIETY. YEAR BOOK. c/o Adriance Memorial Library, Poughkeepsie, NY 12601	L	A	
THE DUTCHESS HISTORIAN. Dutchess County Historical Society, 9 Vassar Street, Poughkeepsie, NY 12601	L	Q	
THE EAST KENTUCKIAN. Henry P. Scalf, ed., Box 107, Stanville, KY 41659	L	Q	
EASTERN NEBRASKA GENEALOGICAL SOCIETY QUARTERLY. 4011 North Somers Street, Fremont, NE 68025	L	Q	
EASTERN WASHINGTON GENEALOGICAL SOCIETY BULLETIN. P.O. Box 1826, Spokane, WA 99210	L	Q	
EAST TEXAS GENEALOGICAL SOCIETY BULLETIN. P.O. Box 851, Tyler, TX 75710	L	Q	
THE ECHOER. Mary Freese Warrell, ed., Wheeling, WV	R	B	
ECHOES. East Tennessee Historical Society, Lawson McGhee Library, Knoxville, TN 37902	L	IR	
END OF THE TRAIL RESEARCHERS. Route 1, Box 138, Lebanon, OR 97355	L	Q	

TITLE OF PERIODICAL, ADDRESS	SCOPE	FREQUENCY OF PUBLICATION	PRIORITY
THE EPISTLE. Rosemary E. Bachelor, ed., P.O. Box 398, Machias, ME 04654 [although this is a family magazine, it has a regular section featuring U.S. genealogical sources]	S/N	Q	
THE ESSEX ANTIQUARIAN. 1897–1909. Sidney Perley, ed., Salem, MA	L	Q	
ESSEX INSTITUTE HISTORICAL COLLECTIONS. 132-34 Essex Street, Salem, MA 01970 (vols. 1-20 reprinted)	R	Q	
THE EXCHANGE: THE GENEALOGICAL PENNY PINCHER'S NEWSLETTER. Mrs. Bette Miller Radewald, ed., 639 Sandalwood Court, Riverside, CA 92507	S	IR	
FALLING LEAVES. 1640 Newport Boulevard, S–41, Costa Mesa, CA 92627	L	Q	
FAMILIES. Ontario Genealogical Society, Box 66, Station Q, Toronto, Ontario M4T 2L7	R	Q	*
FAMILIES OF ANCIENT NEW HAVEN. See THE AMERICAN GENEALOGIST.			
FAMILY FINDINGS. Mid-West Tennessee Genealogical Society, P.O. Box 3175, Murray Station, Jackson, TN 38301	L	Q	
FAMILY PUZZLERS. Heritage Papers. Route 2, Box 86, Danielsville, GA 30633	N	W	**

TITLE OF PERIODICAL, ADDRESS	SCOPE	FREQUENCY OF PUBLICATION	PRIORITY
FAMILY REFERENCE INDEX. Genealogy Inn, P.O. Box 11121, Salt Lake City, UT 84147	S	Q	
FAMILY TRAILS. Michigan Department of Education, State Library Services, 735 East Michigan Avenue, Lansing, MI 48913	L	SA	**
THE FAMILY TREE. Waco McLennan County Library, 1717 Austin Avenue, Waco, TX 76701	L	Q	
THE FAMILY TREE. 1969-70. Genealogical Heritages, Ltd., Denver, CO, and Salt Lake City, UT	I	6/yr	
FAMILY TREE TALKS. Muskegon County Genealogical Society, 3301 Highland, Muskegon Heights, MI 49444	L	Q	
FAULKNER FACTS & FIDDLINGS. Faulkner County Historical Society, P.O. Box 731, Conway, AR 72032	L	Q	
FAYETTE FACTS. Fayette County Genealogical Society, P.O. Box 177, Vandalia, IL 62471	L	Q	
FEDERATION OF GENEALOGICAL SOCIETIES NEWSLETTER. P.O. Box 743, Midlothian, IL 60445	S	IR	
FELLOWSHIP OF BRETHREN GENEALOGISTS NEWSLETTER. Elizabeth Weigle, Secy., 318 Perry Street, Elgin, IL 60120	E	Q	
THE FILSON CLUB HISTORY QUARTERLY. 118 West Breckinridge Street, Louisville, KY 40203	L	Q	

TITLE OF PERIODICAL, ADDRESS	SCOPE	FREQUENCY OF PUBLICATION	PRIORITY
THE FIRELANDS PIONEER. 1858–1937. Firelands Historical Society, Norwalk, OH	L	A	
FLASHBACK. Washington County Historical Society, P.O. Box 357, Fayetteville, AR 72701	L	Q	
FLINT GENEALOGICAL QUARTERLY. Flint Genealogical Society, Inc., 1150 Woodside Drive, Flint, MI 48503	L	Q	
FLORIDA GENEALOGICAL JOURNAL. P.O. Box 18624, Tampa, FL 33679	L	Q	
FOOTPRINTS. Fort Worth Genealogical Society, P.O. Box 864, Ft. Worth, TX 76101	L	Q	
FOREBEARS. See THE AUGUSTAN			
THE FORUM QUARTERLY. See THE TRACKERS			
FOUR STATES GENEALOGIST. Indian Nations Press, 812 Mayo Building, Tulsa, OK 74103	R	Q	
THE FRANKLIN FIREPLACE. Mrs. Robert Williams, 410 8th Street, Terrace, Warrensburg, MO 64093	R	Q	
FRENCH CANADIAN AND ACADIAN GENEALOGICAL REVIEW. Roland-J. Auger, editor-in-chief, Case Postale 845, Haute-Ville, Quebec G1R 4S7	S/I	Q	**

TITLE OF PERIODICAL, ADDRESS	SCOPE	FREQUENCY OF PUBLICATION	PRIORITY
FULTON COUNTY HISTORICAL AND GENEALOGICAL SOCIETY NEWSLETTER. 1040 North Main Street, Canton, IL 61520	L	Q	
GATEWAY TO THE WEST. Anita Short, ed., R.R. 1, Arcanum, OH 45304; and Ruth Bowers, ed., R.R. 3, Box 120, Union City, IN 47390	L	Q	
GEMS OF GENEALOGY. Bay Area Genealogical Society, 832 South Quincy Street, Green Bay, WI 54301	L	6/yr	
THE GENEALOGICAL ACORN. 1968-69. G.A.B. Publications, Inc., Tampa, FL	I	IR	
THE GENEALOGICAL ADVERTISER. 1898-1901. Lucy Hall Greenlaw, Cambridge, MA; Reprint by Genealogical Publishing Co., Baltimore, 1974	R	Q	
GENEALOGICAL AIDS BULLETIN. Miami Valley Genealogical Society, P.O. Box 1364, Dayton, OH 45401	L	Q	
GENEALOGICAL BRANCHES FROM MONROE COUNTY, WISCONSIN. Route 3, Box 177A, Black River Falls, WI 54615	L	Q	
GENEALOGICAL FORUM OF PORT-LAND, OREGON, INC., BULLETIN. 1410 Southwest Morrison, Suite 812, Portland, OR 97205	L	M	
GENEALOGICAL GAZETTE FOR THE BLIND. Genealogical Library for the Blind and Physically Handicapped, Inc., 4176 English Oak Drive, Doraville, GA 30040	S	Q	

Select List of Periodicals

TITLE OF PERIODICAL, ADDRESS	SCOPE	FREQUENCY OF PUBLICATION	PRIORITY
GENEALOGICAL GOLDMINE. Paradise Genealogical Society, P.O. Box 335, Paradise, CA 95969	L	Q	
THE GENEALOGICAL HELPER. Everton Publishers, Inc., P.O. Box 368, Logan, UT 84321	I	B	*
GENEALOGICAL HOBBY MAGAZINE. Chedwato Service, RD 3, Box 120A, Middleboro, MA 02346			
GENEALOGICAL JOURNAL. Utah Genealogical Association, P.O. Box 1144, Salt Lake City, UT 84110	I	Q	*
GENEALOGICAL LIBRARY QUARTERLY. Hartwell Co., 1510 Cravens Avenue, Torrance, CA 90501	S	IR	**
THE GENEALOGICAL MAGAZINE (title varied: THE GENEALOGICAL QUARTERLY MAGAZINE; PUTNAM'S HISTORICAL MAGAZINE). 1905-6. Eben Putnam, Boston, MA	N	M	
THE GENEALOGICAL MAGAZINE OF NEW JERSEY. P.O. Box 1291, New Brunswick, NJ 08903	L	3/yr	**
GENEALOGICAL NEWS WEEKLY. P.O. Box 1775, Opa Locka, FL 33055	N	W	
GENEALOGICAL NEWSLETTER AND RESEARCH AIDS (title varied). 1955-63. Inez Waldenmaier. Washington, D.C. Current Address: 722 North Birmingham Place, Tulsa, OK 74110	N	Q	
GENEALOGICAL PERIODICAL ADVISORY BULLETIN. 1968-73. George Ely Russell, Mitchellville, MD	S	IR	

TITLE OF PERIODICAL, ADDRESS	SCOPE	FREQUENCY OF PUBLICATION	PRIORITY
THE GENEALOGICAL QUARTERLY MAGAZINE. 1900-1905. Eben Putnam, Boston, MA. See THE GENEALOGICAL MAGAZINE	N	M	
THE GENEALOGICAL RECORD. Houston Genealogical Forum, Marolf P. Gregory, ed., 7130 Evans, Houston, TX 77017	L	Q	
GENEALOGICAL REFERENCE BUILDERS "NEWSLETTER." Elaine Walker, ed., P.O. Box 249, Post Falls, ID 83854	N	Q	
GENEALOGICAL REGISTER. See THE LOUISIANA GENEALOGICAL REGISTER			
GENEALOGICAL RESEARCH NEWS (title varied: AMERICAN RIVER GENEALOGICAL LIBRARY NEWSLETTER; SACRAMENTO AREA GENEALOGICAL LIBRARY NEWSLETTER; SACRAMENTO BRANCH GENEALOGICAL LIBRARY NEWSLETTER; SACRAMENTO GENEALOGICAL NEWSLETTER). Sacramento LDS Branch Genealogical Library, 5343 Halsted Avenue, Carmichael, CA 95608	I	M	
THE GENEALOGICAL SOCIETY BULLETIN. 1958-67. Fort Worth Genealogical Society, Ft. Worth, TX	L	IR	
THE GENEALOGICAL SOCIETY OBSERVER. 1956-- . Genealogical Society of The Church of Jesus Christ of Latter-day Saints. 50 East North Temple, Salt Lake City, UT 84150	E/S	IR	

TITLE OF PERIODICAL, ADDRESS	SCOPE	FREQUENCY OF PUBLICATION	PRIORITY
GENEALOGICAL SOCIETY OF GREATER MIAMI. P.O. Box 01-1808, Miami, FL 33132	L	Q	
THE GENEALOGICAL SOCIETY OF OLD TRYON COUNTY, NORTH CAROLINA. THE BULLETIN. P.O. Box 745, Spindale, NC 28160	L	Q	
GENEALOGICAL SOCIETY OF PENNSYLVANIA. PUBLICATIONS. See THE PENNSYLVANIA GENEA-LOGICAL MAGAZINE			
GENEALOGICAL TIPS. Tip-o'-Texas Genealogical Society, Harlingen Public Library, 502 East Tyler, Harlingen, TX 78550	L	Q	
THE GENEALOGIST. Ray Bakehorn, ed., R.R. 3, Kokomo, IN 46901	N	Q	
THE GENEALOGIST'S POST. Richard T. and Mildred C. Williams, Dansboro, PA	N	Q	
GENEALOGY. Willard Heiss, ed., Indiana Historical Society, 315 West Ohio Street, Indianapolis, IN 46202	N	8/yr	*
GENEALOGY: A JOURNAL OF AMERICAN ANCESTRY. 1910-16. William M. Clemens, publisher, New York, NY	N	M	
GENEALOGY AND HERALDRY. International Society of Heraldry and Family Trees, Box 1717, Washington, DC 20013	S	Q	
GENEALOGY & HISTORY. 1940-64. Adrian Ely Mount, Washington, DC	N/S	Q	

TITLE OF PERIODICAL, ADDRESS	SCOPE	FREQUENCY OF PUBLICATION	PRIORITY
THE GENEALOGY BUG (formerly THE MARTIN GENEALOGIST). P.O. Box 155, North English, IA 52316	N	M	
THE GENEALOGY CLUB OF AMERICA MAGAZINE. See GENEALOGY DIGEST; title changed with vol. 5, no. 3, Fall 1974	I	Q	
GENEALOGY DIGEST (formerly THE GENEALOGY CLUB OF AMERICA MAGAZINE). 5450 South Green Street, Salt Lake City, UT 84107	I	B	
THE GENIE. Ark-La-Tex Genealogical Association, P.O. Box 4462, Shreveport, LA 71104	R	Q	
GENIE BUG. North Central Iowa Genealogical Society, Route 3, 35th Street, N.E., Mason City, IA 50401	L	Q	
THE GEORGIA GENEALOGICAL MAGAZINE. Georgia Genealogical Reprints, c/o Rev. Silas Emmett Lucas, Jr., P.O. Box 738, Easley, SC 29640	L	Q	
THE GEORGIA GENEALOGICAL SOCIETY QUARTERLY. P.O. Box 38066, Atlanta, GA 30334	L	Q	
THE GEORGIA GENEALOGIST. Heritage Papers, Route 2, Box 86, Danielsville, GA 30633	L	Q	
GEORGIA MAGAZINE. Ann E. Lewis, P.O. Box 4047, Decatur, GA	L	B	
GEORGIA PIONEERS GENEALOGICAL MAGAZINE. Mary Carter, ed., P.O. Box 1028, Albany, GA 31702	L	Q	

TITLE OF PERIODICAL, ADDRESS	SCOPE	FREQUENCY OF PUBLICATION	PRIORITY
THE GEORGIA RESEARCHER. 1963. Allstates Research Co., Murray, UT	L	Q	
THE GERMAN-AMERICAN GENEA-LOGIST. Institute for German-American Studies, 21010 Mastick Road, Cleveland, OH 44126	E/S	Q	**
GERMAN-AMERICAN STUDIES. Institute for German-American Studies, 21010 Mastick Road, Cleveland, OH 44126	E/S	SA	
GLEANINGS FROM THE HEART OF THE CORNBELT. Bloomington-Normal Genealogical Society, P.O. Box 488, Normal, IL 61761	L	Q	
GOSHEN TRAILS. Hamilton County Historical Society, 209 West 1st, Danville, IL 61832	L	Q	
THE GREENE HILLS ECHO. Greene County Historical Society, RD 2, Waynesburg, PA 15370	L	Q	
GWINNETT HISTORICAL SOCIETY NEWSLETTER. P.O. Box 261, Lawrenceville, GA 30245	L	Q	
THE HAPPY HUNTER. Cumberland County Genealogical Society, P.O. Box 676, Greenup, IL 62428	L	Q	
HAWKEYE HERITAGE. Iowa Genea-logical Society, P.O. Box 3815, Des Moines, IA 50322	L	Q	
HAYS COUNTY HISTORICAL AND GENEALOGICAL SOCIETY, INC. QUARTERLY. P.O. Box 1387, San Marcos, TX 78666	L	Q	

TITLE OF PERIODICAL, ADDRESS	SCOPE	FREQUENCY OF PUBLICATION	PRIORITY
THE HEADHUNTER. TRW Genealogical Society, One Space Park, S/1435, Redondo Beach, CA 90278	L	Q	
HEART OF TEXAS RECORDS. Central Texas Genealogical Society, 1717 Austin Avenue, Waco, TX 76701	L	Q	
THE HERALDIC JOURNAL. 1865–68. Reprint: Baltimore: Genealogical Publishing Co., 1972	S	IR	
HERALDRY. Hartwell Co., 1510 Cravens Avenue, Torrance, CA 90501	S	IR	
HERALDRY IN CANADA. Heraldry Society of Canada, 900 Pinecrest Road, Ottawa, Ontario K2B 6B3	S	IR	
THE HERITAGE. Crawford County Historical Society, c/o Mrs. James E. West, 3201 South Dallas, Ft. Smith, AR 72901	L	Q	
THE HERITAGE GENEALOGICAL SOCIETY QUARTERLY. P.O. Box 73, Neodesha, KS 66757	L	Q	
HERITAGE REVIEW. North Dakota Historical Society of Germans from Russia, Box 1671, Bismarck, ND 58501	S	SA	
HISTORICAL METHODS NEWSLETTER. UCIS Publications, G-6 Mervis Hall, University of Pittsburgh, Pittsburgh, PA 15260	S/N	Q	
HISTORICAL WYOMING. Wyoming County Historian's Office, 143 North Main Street, Warsaw, NY 14569	L	Q	

Select List of Periodicals

TITLE OF PERIODICAL, ADDRESS	SCOPE	FREQUENCY OF PUBLICATION	PRIORITY
HISTORY TRAILS. Baltimore County Historical Society, 9811 Van Buren Lane, Cockeysville, MD 21030	L	Q	
THE HOOSIER GENEALOGIST. Indiana Historical Society, 315 West Ohio Street, Indianapolis, IN 46202	L	Q	**
THE HOUSTON GENEALOGICAL RECORD. Houston Genealogical Forum, 7130 Evans Street, Houston, TX 77017	L	Q	
THE HUXFORD GENEALOGICAL SOCIETY QUARTERLY. P.O. Box 116, Homerville, GA 31634	L	Q	
THE ICELANDIC CANADIAN. c/o Harold Johnson, 868 Arlington Street, Winnipeg, Manitoba R3E 2E4	S	Q	
THE IDAHO GENEALOGICAL SOCIETY QUARTERLY. 325 State Street, Boise, ID 83702	L	Q	
THE ILL-IA-MO SEARCHER. Mrs. Judy Sheffler, R.R. 1, Warsaw, IL 62379	L	Q	
THE ILLIANA GENEALOGIST. Illiana Genealogical and Historical Society, P.O. Box 207, Danville, IL 61832	L	Q	**
ILLINOIS LIBRARIES. Illinois State Library, Springfield, IL 62756	L	10/yr	
ILLINOIS STATE GENEALOGICAL SOCIETY QUARTERLY. P.O. Box 2225, Springfield, IL 62705	L	Q	**

TITLE OF PERIODICAL, ADDRESS	SCOPE	FREQUENCY OF PUBLICATION	PRIORITY
THE INDEPENDENCE COUNTY CHRONICLE. Independence County Historical Society, Box 2036, Batesville, AR 72501	L	Q	
INTERNATIONAL FINDERS. 1965-66. International Genealogical and Biographical Society, Provo, UT	I	IR	
IROQUOIS COUNTY HISTORICAL SOCIETY NEWSLETTER. 103 West Cherry Street, Watseka, IL 60970	L	Q	
THE IROQUOIS STALKER. Iroquois County Genealogical Society, Old Courthouse Museum, 103 West Cherry Street, Watseka, IL 60970	L	Q	
JACKSONVILLE GENEALOGICAL JOURNAL. Jacksonville Area Genealogical Society, P.O. Box 21, Jacksonville, IL 62650	L	IR	
JACKSONVILLE GENEALOGICAL SOCIETY MAGAZINE. P.O. Box 7076, Jacksonville, FL 32210	L	A	
JEFFERSON COUNTY HISTORICAL SOCIETY MAGAZINE. Charles Town, WV 25414	L	A	
THE JOHNSON COUNTY GENEALOGIST. Johnson County Genealogical Society, Inc., P.O. Box 8057, Shawnee Mission, KS 66208	L	Q	
THE JOURNAL OF AMERICAN GENEALOGY. 1921-30. National Historical Society, Washington, DC	N	Q	
THE JOURNAL OF AMERICAN HISTORY. 1907-33. National Historical Society, Washington, DC	N	Q	

TITLE OF PERIODICAL, ADDRESS	SCOPE	FREQUENCY OF PUBLICATION	PRIORITY
JOURNAL OF FAMILY HISTORY. National Council on Family Relations, 1219 University Avenue, Southeast, Minneapolis, MN 55414	S	Q	
JOURNAL OF GENEALOGY. Anderson Publishing Co., P.O. Box 31097, Omaha, NE 68131	I	M	*
JOURNAL OF GERMAN-AMERICAN STUDIES. See GERMAN-AMERICAN STUDIES			
JOURNAL OF NORTH CAROLINA GENEALOGY. See NORTH CAROLINA GENEALOGY			
JOURNAL OF THE AMERICAN COLLEGE OF HERALDRY. Dr. David P. Johnson, Pres., Drawer CG, University, AL 35486	S	IR	
THE KALAMAZOO VALLEY FAMILY NEWSLETTER. Kalamazoo Valley Genealogical Society, 315 South Rose Street, Kalamazoo, MI 49006	L	Q	
KANHISTIQUE. Box 8, Ellsworth, KS 67439	L	M	
THE KANSAS CITY GENEALOGIST. Heart of America Genealogical Society, c/o Kansas City Public Library, 311 East 12th Street, Kansas City, MO 64106	L	Q	
KANSAS KIN. Riley County Genealogical Society, 2224 Stone Post Road, Manhattan, KS 66502	L	Q	
KENTUCKY ANCESTORS. Kentucky Historical Society, P.O. Box H, Frankfort, KY 40601	L	Q	

TITLE OF PERIODICAL, ADDRESS	SCOPE	FREQUENCY OF PUBLICATION	PRIORITY
KENTUCKY FAMILY RECORDS. West-Central Kentucky Family Research Association, P.O. Box 1465, Owensboro, KY 42301	L	10/yr	
THE KENTUCKY GENEALOGIST. Martha Porter Miller, ed., Box 4894, Washington, DC 20008	L	Q	**
THE KENTUCKY RESEARCHER. Discontinued. Allstates Research Co., West Jordan, UT	L	Q	
KERN-GEN. Kern County Genealogical Society, P.O. Box 2214, Bakersfield, CA 93303	L	Q	
KEYHOLE. Genealogical Society of Southwestern Pennsylvania, Citizens Library, 55 South College, Washington, PA 15301	L	Q	
KEYSTONE KUZZINS. Erie Society for Genealogical Research, P.O. Box 1403, Erie, PA 16512	L	Q	
KNOX COUNTY ILLINOIS GENEALOGICAL SOCIETY QUARTERLY. P.O. Box 13, Galesburg, IL 61401	L	Q	
LANE COUNTY HISTORICAL SOCIETY NEWSLETTER. 89239 Old Coburg Road, Eugene, OR 97401	L	Q	
LAUREL MESSENGER. Historical and Genealogical Society of Somerset County, Pennsylvania, Box 533, Somerset, PA 15501	L	Q	
LEAVES AND SAPLINGS. See SAN DIEGO LEAVES AND SAPLINGS			

TITLE OF PERIODICAL, ADDRESS	SCOPE	FREQUENCY OF PUBLICATION	PRIORITY
LE MOIS GENEALOGIQUE. Discontinued. La Societe Genealogique Canadienne-Francaise, Montreal, Quebec	L	M	
LES CAHIERS. La Societe Historique Acadienne, Case Postale 2363, Station A, Moncton, New Brunswick E1C 8J3	L	Q	
LIFELINER. Genealogical Society of Riverside, P.O. Box 2557, Riverside, CA 92506	N	Q	
LINCOLN COUNTY TENNESSEE PIONEERS. Jane Warren Waller, 131 Woodhaven Lane, Seabrook, TX 77586	L	Q	
THE LIVING TREE NEWS. Harris County Genealogical Society, P.O. Box 3329, Pasadena, TX 77501	L	Q	
LOCAL HISTORY & GENEALOGICAL SOCIETY. See THE QUARTERLY			
LOST IN CANADA? CANADIAN-AMERICAN QUERY EXCHANGE. Mrs. Joy Reisinger, 1020 Central Avenue, Sparta, WI 54656	S/R	Q	**
THE LOUISIANA GENEALOGICAL REGISTER (formerly GENEALOGICAL REGISTER). Louisiana Genealogical and Historical Society, P.O. Box 3454, Baton Rouge, LA 70821	L	Q	
THE LOYALIST GAZETTE. United Empire Loyalists' Association of Canada, 23 Prince Arthur Avenue, Toronto, Ontario M5R 1B2	S	SA	

TITLE OF PERIODICAL, ADDRESS	SCOPE	FREQUENCY OF PUBLICATION	PRIORITY
MAGAZINE OF BIBLIOGRAPHIES. 1209 Clover Lane, Ft. Worth, TX 76107	N	IR	
MAGAZINE OF NEW ENGLAND HISTORY. 1891-93.	R	Q	
MAINE GENEALOGICAL INQUIRER. Mr. and Mrs. Michael J. Denis, P.O. Box 253, Oakland, ME 04963	L	B	
THE MAINE HISTORICAL AND GENEALOGICAL RECORDER. 1884-98. S. M. Watson, Portland, ME (reprinted in 3 vols.)	R	IR	
THE MAINE HISTORICAL MAGAZINE (formerly THE BANGOR HISTORICAL MAGAZINE). 1885-95. Joseph W. Porter, Bangor, ME	L	M	
MAINE OLD CEMETERY ASSOCIATION NEWSLETTER. c/o Amanda L. Bond, 8 Greenway Avenue, Springvale, ME 04083	S/L	Q	
THE MARTIN GENEALOGIST. See THE GENEALOGY BUG			
THE MARYLAND AND DELAWARE GENEALOGIST. Raymond B. Clark, Jr., and Sara Seth Clark, eds., Box 352, St. Michaels, MD 21663	L	Q	**
MARYLAND GENEALOGICAL SOCIETY BULLETIN. 201 West Monument Street, Baltimore, MD 21201	I	Q	
MARYLAND GENEALOGICAL SOCIETY NEWSLETTER. 201 West Monument Street, Baltimore, MD 21201	L	Q	

TITLE OF PERIODICAL, ADDRESS	SCOPE	FREQUENCY OF PUBLICATION	PRIORITY
THE MARYLAND HISTORICAL AND GENEALOGICAL BULLETIN. 1930– 50. Robert F. Hayes, Jr., Baltimore, MD	L	Q	
MARYLAND HISTORICAL MAGA- ZINE. 201 West Monument Street, Baltimore, MD 21201	L	Q	
THE MASSACHUSETTS MAGAZINE. 1908–18. Salem Press Co., Salem, MA. Reprint in 5 vols., Johnson Reprint Corp., New York, 1967.	R	Q	
MASSOG. Massachusetts Society of Genealogists, P.O. Box 215, Ashland, MA 01721	L	Q	
THE MAYFLOWER DESCENDANT. 1899–1937. Original title discon- tinued. (See THE MAYFLOWER QUARTERLY). Massachusetts Society of Mayflower Descendants, Boston, MA	S/L	Q	
THE MAYFLOWER QUARTERLY. General Society of Mayflower Des- cendants, 128 Massasoit Drive, Warwick, RI 02888	S	Q	**
M.C.G.S. REPORTER. Milwaukee County Genealogical Society, Inc., 916 East Lyon Street, Milwaukee, WI 53202	L	Q	
MEMOIRES. Societe Genealogique Canadienne-Francaise, Case Postale 335, Place d'Armes, Montreal, Que- bec H2Y 3H1	L	3/yr	
MENNONITE HERITAGE. Arthur W. Nafziger, IMHGS, 600 East 2d Street, Hopedale, IL 61747	E	Q	

TITLE OF PERIODICAL, ADDRESS	SCOPE	FREQUENCY OF PUBLICATION	PRIORITY
MENNONITE HISTORICAL BULLETIN. 1940–59. Mennonite General Conference, Scottdale, PA 15683	E	Q	
THE MENNONITE QUARTERLY REVIEW. Mennonite Historical Society, Goshen College, Goshen, IN 46526	S/E	Q	
MENNONITE RESEARCH JOURNAL. Lancaster Mennonite Conference Historical Society, 2215 Millstream Road, Lancaster, PA 17602	E	Q	
MESQUITE HISTORICAL AND GENEALOGICAL SOCIETY. QUARTERLY. P.O. Box 165, Mesquite, TX 75149	L	Q	
THE MESQUITE TREE (cover title). See MESQUITE HISTORICAL AND GENEALOGICAL SOCIETY QUARTERLY			
MICHIANA SEARCHER. Elkhart County Genealogical Library, 1812 Jeanwood Drive, Elkhart, IN 46514	L	Q	
MICHIGAN HERITAGE. Dr. Ethel W. Williams, Kalamazoo, MI	L	Q	
MICHIGANA. Western Michigan Genealogical Society, Grand Rapids Public Library, Library Plaza, N.E., Grand Rapids, MI 49502	L	Q	
MID-HUDSON GENEALOGICAL JOURNAL. 1112 Pond Drive, West Columbia, SC 29169	L	Q	
MID-HUDSON GENEALOGICAL JOURNAL. 20 Styvestandt Drive, Poughkeepsie, NY 12601	L	Q	

TITLE OF PERIODICAL, ADDRESS	SCOPE	FREQUENCY OF PUBLICATION	PRIORITY
MIDWEST GENEALOGICAL REGISTER. Midwest Genealogical Society, Inc., Box 1121, Wichita, KS 67201	R	Q	**
MIDWESTERN HERITAGE. Janlen Enterprises, 2236 South 77th Street, West Allis, WI 53219	R	Q	**
MINNESOTA GENEALOGICAL SOCIETY NEWSLETTER. P.O. Box 16006, St. Paul, MN 55105	L	Q	
MINNESOTA GENEALOGIST. Minnesota Genealogical Society, P.O. Box 16006, St. Paul, MN 55105	L	Q	
MISSING LINKS. 1962–66. Chedwato Service, Burlington, VT	S	M	
MISSISSINEWA GENEALOGICAL QUARTERLY. Ray Bakehorn, ed., R.R. 3, Box 292, Kokomo, IN 46901	L	Q	
MISSISSIPPI COAST HISTORICAL AND GENEALOGICAL SOCIETY. PROCEEDINGS AND JOURNAL. P.O. Box 513, Biloxi, MS 39530	L	Q	
MISSISSIPPI GENEALOGICAL EXCHANGE. Richard S. Lackey, P.O. Box 434, Forest, MS 39074	L	Q	
MISSISSIPPI GENEALOGY AND LOCAL HISTORY. Norman E. Gillis, ed., P.O. Box 9114, Shreveport, LA 71109	L	Q	
MISSOURI HISTORICAL REVIEW. State Historical Society of Missouri, 5601 Paris Road, Columbia, MO 65201	L	Q	

TITLE OF PERIODICAL, ADDRESS	SCOPE	FREQUENCY OF PUBLICATION	PRIORITY
MISSOURI PIONEERS. Nadine Hodges and Mrs. Howard W. Woodruff, 1824 South Harvard, Independence, MO 64052	L	SA	
THE MISSOURI RESEARCHER. Discontinued. Allstates Research Co., West Jordan, UT	L	Q	
THE MOJAVA NUGGET. Mojava Desert Genealogical Society, P.O. Box 1320, Barstow, CA 92311	L	Q	
THE MONTGOMERY COUNTY GENEALOGICAL JOURNAL. Ann Evans Alley, Route 1, Box 76, Adams, TN 37010	L	Q	
MOULTRIE COUNTY HERITAGE. Moultrie County Historical and Genealogical Society, P.O. Box MM, Sullivan, IL 61951	L	Q	
MOULTRIE COUNTY HISTORICAl AND GENEALOGICAL SOCIETY NEWSLETTER. P.O. Box MM, Sullivan, IL 61951	L	Q	
THE MT. HOOD TRACKERS. See THE TRACKERS			
THE NAME TRACER. Las Vegas Branch Genealogical Library, 509 South 9th Street, Las Vegas, NV 89101	L	Q	
NAMES IN SOUTH CAROLINA. Department of English, University of South Carolina, Columbia, SC 29208	S/L	A	

TITLE OF PERIODICAL, ADDRESS	SCOPE	FREQUENCY OF PUBLICATION	PRIORITY
NAMES: JOURNAL OF THE AMERICAN NAME SOCIETY. English Department, State University College, Potsdam, NY 13676	S	Q	
THE NARRAGANSETT HISTORICAL REGISTER. 1882-91, ed. by James N. Arnold, 9 vols., Narragansett Historical Publishing Co., Providence, RI	L	Q	
NATIONAL GENEALOGICAL SOCIETY NEWSLETTER. 1921 Sunderland Place, N.W., Washington, DC 20036	N	Q	*
NATIONAL GENEALOGICAL SOCIETY QUARTERLY. 1921 Sunderland Place, N.W., Washington, DC 20036	N	Q	*
THE NEBRASKA AND MIDWEST GENEALOGICAL RECORD. Raymond E. Dale, Lincoln, NE	R	Q	
THE NEW BRUNSWICK MAGAZINE. 1898-99. New Brunswick Historical Society, St. John, New Brunswick	L	IR	
THE NEW ENGLAND HISTORICAL AND GENEALOGICAL REGISTER. 101 Newbury Street, Boston, MA 02116	R	Q	*
THE NEW HAMPSHIRE GENEALOGICAL RECORD. 1904-10. Charles W. Tibbetts, ed., Dover, NH	L	Q	
THE NEW HAVEN GENEALOGICAL MAGAZINE (vols. 1-8). See THE AMERICAN GENEALOGIST	R	Q	

TITLE OF PERIODICAL, ADDRESS	SCOPE	FREQUENCY OF PUBLICATION	PRIORITY
THE NEW JERSEY GENESIS. 151 East 81st Street, New York, NY 10028	L	Q	
NEW MEXICO GENEALOGIST. New Mexico Genealogical Society, P.O. Box 8734, Albuquerque, NM 87108	L	Q	
NEW ORLEANS GENESIS. Genealogical Research Society of New Orleans, P.O. Box 51791, New Orleans, LA 70151	R	Q	
NEWPORT HISTORICAL MAGAZINE. See THE RHODE ISLAND HISTORICAL MAGAZINE			
NEWS AND JOURNAL. Tippah County Historical and Genealogical Society, Ripley, MS 38663	L	Q	
NEWS 'N' NOTES. St. Louis Genealogical Society, 1695 South Brentwood Boulevard, Suite 203, St. Louis, MO 63144	L	Q	
NEWSLEAF. Ontario Genealogical Society, Box 66, Station Q, Toronto, Ontario M4T 2L7	L	IR	
THE NEW YORK GENEALOGICAL AND BIOGRAPHICAL RECORD. 122 East 58th Street, New York, NY 10022	L/R	Q	*
THE NORTH CAROLINA GENEALOGICAL SOCIETY JOURNAL. P.O. Box 1492, Raleigh, NC 27602	L	Q	

Select List of Periodicals

TITLE OF PERIODICAL, ADDRESS	SCOPE	FREQUENCY OF PUBLICATION	PRIORITY
NORTH CAROLINA GENEALOGY (formerly JOURNAL OF NORTH CAROLINA GENEALOGY). William Perry Johnson, ed., P.O. Box 1770, Raleigh, NC 27602	L	SA	
THE NORTH CAROLINA HISTORICAL AND GENEALOGICAL REGISTER. 1900–03. J.R.B. Hathaway, Edenton, NC; Indexed by Worth S. Ray	L	Q	
THE NORTH CAROLINA HISTORICAL REVIEW. Division of Archives and History, 109 East Jones Street, Raleigh, NC 27611	L	Q	
THE NORTH CAROLINIAN. William Perry Johnson, ed., Box 531, Raleigh, NC	L	Q	
NORTH PLATTE GENEALOGICAL SOCIETY. QUARTERLY. 820 West 4th Street, North Platte, NE 69101	L	Q	
NORTH STAR NUGGETS. Fairbanks Genealogical Society, 1552 Noble Street, Fairbanks, AK 99701	L	Q	
NORTH TEXAS PIONEER. North Texas Genealogical and Historical Association, Wichita Falls, TX	L	Q	
NORTHEAST ALABAMA SETTLERS. Northeast Alabama Genealogical Society, Inc., P.O. Box 674, Gadsden, AL 35902	L	Q	
NORTHEAST LOUISIANA GENEALOGICAL SOCIETY. P.O. Box 2743, Monroe, LA 71201	L	Q	

TITLE OF PERIODICAL, ADDRESS	SCOPE	FREQUENCY OF PUBLICATION	PRIORITY
THE NORTHEAST TEXAS GENEA-LOGICAL SOCIETY QUARTERLY. P.O. Box 458, Mineola, TX 75773	L	Q	
NORTHAMPTON COUNTY COUSINS. Mrs. Taney Brazeal, ed., Route 3, Box 14, Fairhope, AL 36532	L	Q	
NORTHLAND NEWSLETTER. Range Genealogical Society, Box 726, Buhl, MN 55713	L	Q	
NORTHWEST GEORGIA HISTORICAL AND GENEALOGICAL SOCIETY QUARTERLY. Box 2484, Rome, GA 30161	L	Q	
THE NOVA SCOTIA HISTORICAL QUARTERLY. P.O. Box 1102, Halifax, Nova Scotia	L	Q	
NOW AND THEN. Muncy Historical Society and Museum of History, Muncy, PA 17756	L	Q	
THE NUTMEGGER. See THE CON-NECTICUT NUTMEGGER			
THE OHIO GENEALOGICAL QUAR-TERLY. 1937–43. Columbus Genea-logical Society, Columbus, OH	L	Q	
OHIO GENEALOGICAL SOCIETY. NEWSLETTER. P.O. Box 2625, Mansfield, OH 44906	L	M	
OHIO RECORDS AND PIONEER FAMILIES. Ohio Genealogical So-ciety, 454 Park Avenue West, Mans-field, OH 44906	L	Q	**

TITLE OF PERIODICAL, ADDRESS	SCOPE	FREQUENCY OF PUBLICATION	PRIORITY
THE OHIO RESEARCHER. 1962. Allstates Research Co., West Jordan, UT	L	Q	
OKLAHOMA GENEALOGICAL SOCIETY BULLETIN. See OKLAHOMA GENEALOGICAL SOCIETY QUARTERLY			
OKLAHOMA GENEALOGICAL SOCIETY QUARTERLY (formerly OKLAHOMA GENEALOGICAL SOCIETY BULLETIN). P.O. Box 314, Oklahoma City, OK 73101	L	Q	
THE 'OLD NORTHWEST' GENEALOGICAL QUARTERLY. 1898-1912. Old Northwest Genealogical Society, Columbus, OH	L	Q	
OLYMPIA GENEALOGICAL SOCIETY QUARTERLY. 7th and Franklin Streets, Olympia, WA 98501	L	Q	
ONTARIO GENEALOGICAL SOCIETY. BRANCH NEWS. Ottawa Branch, Ontario Genealogical Society, P.O. Box 8346, Ottawa, Ontario K1G 3H8	L	Q	
THE ONTARIO GENEALOGICAL SOCIETY BULLETIN. 1962-70. Superseded by FAMILIES	R	IR	
THE ONTARIO REGISTER. Thomas B. Wilson, Lambertville, NJ	L	Q	
ORANGE COUNTY CALIFORNIA GENEALOGICAL SOCIETY QUARTERLY. P.O. Box 1587, Orange, CA 92668	L	Q	

TITLE OF PERIODICAL, ADDRESS	SCOPE	FREQUENCY OF PUBLICATION	PRIORITY
ORANGE COUNTY GENEALOGICAL SOCIETY. P.O. Box 112, Chester, NY 10918	L	Q	
ORANGEBURG HISTORICAL AND GENEALOGICAL RECORD. Box 1616, College Station, Orangeburg, SC 29115	L	Q	
OREGON. End of Trail Researchers, Route 1, Box 138, Lebanon, OR 97355	L	Q	
OREGON GENEALOGICAL SOCIETY BULLETIN. P.O. Box 1214, Eugene, OR 97401	L	IR	
OTTAWA BRANCH NEWS. Ottawa Branch, Ontario Genealogical Society, P.O. Box 8346, Ottawa, Ontario K1G 3H8	L	M	
OUR FAMILY HERITAGE. Genealogical Research, 322 State Street, Fairborn, OH 45324	R	Q	
OUR HERITAGE. San Antonio Genealogical and Historical Society, P.O. Box 5907, San Antonio, TX 78201	L	Q	
THE OZARK QUARTERLY. 1969-73. William A. Yates, Sparta, MO (See THE RIDGE RUNNERS)	L	Q	
THE PALATINE IMMIGRANT. Palatines to America, 157 North State Street, Salt Lake City, UT 84103	S	Q	
PARADISE GENEALOGICAL SOCIETY. P.O. Box 335, Paradise, CA 95969	L	Q	
THE PASTFINDER. Genealogical Association of Southwestern Michigan, P.O. Box 573, St. Joseph, MI 49085	L	Q	

Select List of Periodicals

TITLE OF PERIODICAL, ADDRESS	SCOPE	FREQUENCY OF PUBLICATION	PRIORITY
PEA RIVER TRAILS. Pea River Historical and Genealogical Society, P.O. Box 628, Enterprise, AL 36330	L	SA	
PENNSYLVANIA FOLKLIFE. Box 1053, Lancaster, PA 17604	S/L	Q	
THE PENNSYLVANIA GENEALOGICAL MAGAZINE (formerly PUBLICATIONS). Genealogical Society of Pennsylvania, 1300 Locust Street, Philadelphia, PA 19107	L/R	Q	*
PENNSYLVANIA GENEALOGY MAGAZINE. Mary Lontz, 608 Broadway, Milton, PA 17847	L	Q	
PENNSYLVANIA HERITAGE. Pennsylvania Historical and Museum Commission, Box 1026, Harrisburg, PA 17120	L	Q	
THE PENNSYLVANIA MAGAZINE OF HISTORY AND BIOGRAPHY. Historical Society of Pennsylvania, 1300 Locust Street, Philadelphia, PA 19107	L	Q	
THE PENNSYLVANIA TRAVELER--POST. Richard T. and Mildred C. Williams, P.O. Box 307, Danboro, PA 18916	L	Q	
PILGRIM NOTES AND QUERIES. 1913-17. Massachusetts Society of Mayflower Descendants, Boston, MA	L	IR	
PIONEER. See THE BENTON COUNTY PIONEER			
THE PIONEER. Pioneer Historical Society of Bedford County, Box 571, Bedford, PA 15522	L	Q	

TITLE OF PERIODICAL, ADDRESS	SCOPE	FREQUENCY OF PUBLICATION	PRIORITY
PIONEER HERITANCE. Gene Price, ed., 70 Hillcrest Avenue, Larchmont, NY 10538	L	IR	
PIONEER PATHFINDER. Sioux Valley Genealogical Society, P.O. Box 655, Sioux Falls, SD 57101	L	Q	
PIONEER TRAILS. Birmingham Genealogical Society, Inc., 1028 Montclair Road, Birmingham, AL 35213	L	Q	
PLYMOUTH COLONY GENEALOGICAL HELPER. See THE PLYMOUTH COLONY GENEALOGIST			
THE PLYMOUTH COLONY GENEALOGIST. Hartwell Co., 1510 Cravens Avenue, Torrance, CA 90501	S/L	Q	**
POLISH FAMILY TREE SURNAMES. Thaddeus J. Obal, 739 Hillsdale Avenue, Hillsdale, NJ 07642	E	IR	
POMONA GENEALOGICAL SOCIETY. 714 South Hillward Avenue, West Covina, CA 91791	L	Q	
THE PONTOTOC COUNTY QUARTERLY. Pontotoc County Historical and Genealogical Society, 221 West 16th, Ada, OK 74820	L	Q	
POPE COUNTY HISTORICAL ASSOCIATION QUARTERLY. Pope County Historical Association of Russellville, Arkansas, Inc., 4200 A Street, Little Rock, AR 72205	L	Q	
THE PRAIRIE GLEANER. West Central Missouri Genealogical Society and Library, Inc., Twin Cedars, R.R. 3, Warrensburg, MO 64093	L	Q	

TITLE OF PERIODICAL, ADDRESS	SCOPE	FREQUENCY OF PUBLICATION	PRIORITY
PRAIRIE ROOTS. Peoria County Genealogical Society, P.O. Box 1489, Peoria, IL 61602	L	Q	
PRINCE GEORGE'S COUNTY GENE-ALOGICAL SOCIETY BULLETIN. Box 819, Bowie, MD 20715	L	10/yr	
PROCEEDINGS OF THE AMERICAN ANTIQUARIAN SOCIETY. 185 Salisbury Street, Worcester, MA 01609	S	SA	
PROLOGUE: THE JOURNAL OF THE NATIONAL ARCHIVES. National Archives (GSA), Washington, DC 20408	N	Q	*
THE PROSPECTOR. Clark County, Nevada, Genealogical Society, 4333 El Cid Circle, Las Vegas, NV 89121	L	Q	
PULASKI COUNTY HISTORICAL REVIEW. P.O. Box 653, Little Rock, AR 72203	L	Q	
PUTNAM'S HISTORICAL MAGAZINE. 1892-99. Eben Putnam, Danvers, MA. See THE GENEALOGICAL MAGAZINE	N	M	
THE QUAKER YEOMEN. James E. Bellarts, 7030 Southwest Canyon Road, Portland, OR 97225	E	Q	
THE QUARTERLY (formerly LOCAL HISTORY AND GENEALOGICAL SOCIETY QUARTERLY). Dallas Genealogical Society, P.O. Box 12648, Dallas, TX 75225	N	Q	**

TITLE OF PERIODICAL, ADDRESS	SCOPE	FREQUENCY OF PUBLICATION	PRIORITY
THE QUARTERLY REVIEW. Eastern North Carolina Genealogical Society, P.O. Box 395, New Bern, NC 28560	L	Q	
QUICKSILVER DIGGIN'S. Bonsal-Robinson-Monson, 7554 Normandy Way, San Jose, CA 95129	L	Q	
RECORD ROUNDUP. See WORLD RECORDS			
REDWOOD RESEARCHER. Redwood Genealogical Society, Inc., Box 645, Fortuna, CA 95540	L	Q	
THE REFLECTOR. Amarillo Genealogical Society, P.O. Box 2171, Amarillo, TX	L	Q	
THE REGISTER OF THE KENTUCKY HISTORICAL SOCIETY. P.O. Box H, Frankfort, KY 40601	L	Q	
RELATIVELY SPEAKING. Alberta Genealogical Society, P.O. Box 3151, Station A, Edmonton, Alberta T5J 2G7	L	Q	
THE REPORT. Ohio Genealogical Society, P.O. Box 2625, Mansfield, OH 44906	L	Q	**
THE RESEARCHER. 1926-28. Robert Armistead Stewart, ed., Richmond, VA	R	Q	
THE RESEARCHER. Elizabeth Prather Ellsberry, ed., Box 206, Chillicothe, MO 64601	R	6/yr	
THE RESEARCHER. Tacoma Genealogical Society, P.O. Box 11232, Tacoma, WA 98411	L	Q	

Select List of Periodicals

TITLE OF PERIODICAL, ADDRESS	SCOPE	FREQUENCY OF PUBLICATION	PRIORITY
THE RHODE ISLAND HISTORICAL MAGAZINE (formerly THE NEWPORT HISTORICAL MAGAZINE, ed. by R.H. Tilley). 1880–87. 7 vols., Newport Historical Publishing Co., Newport, RI	L	Q	
RHODE ISLAND HISTORICAL SOCIETY COLLECTIONS. 1827–1941. Rhode Island Historical Society, Providence, RI	L	Q	
R.I. ROOTS. Rhode Island Genealogical Society, Box 207, Mapleville, RI 02839	L	Q	
THE RIDGE RUNNERS. William A. Yates, P.O. Box 7151, Murray, UT 84107	R	Q	**
THE RIVER COUNTIES QUARTERLY. Jill K. Garrett, ed., 610 Terrace Drive, Columbia, TN 38401	L	Q	
THE ROADRUNNER. Chaparral Genealogical Society, P.O. Box 606, Tomball, TX 77375	L	Q	
ROGUE DIGGER (formerly THE ROGUE VALLEY GENEALOGICAL SOCIETY QUARTERLY). P.O. Box 628, Ashland, OR 97520	L	Q	
THE ROGUE VALLEY GENEALOGICAL SOCIETY QUARTERLY. See ROGUE DIGGER.			
ST. LOUIS GENEALOGICAL SOCIETY QUARTERLY. 1617 South Brentwood Boulevard, Room 261, St. Louis, MO 63144	L	Q	

TITLE OF PERIODICAL, ADDRESS	SCOPE	FREQUENCY OF PUBLICATION	PRIORITY
SAGA OF SOUTHERN ILLINOIS. Genealogical Society of Southern Illinois, c/o Mrs. Elizabeth Leighty, 511 West College Street, Carbondale, IL 62901	L	Q	
SAINTS OR HORSE THIEVES? Genealogical Bi-Ways, 1420 Roma Lane, Ft. Worth, TX 76134	R	Q	
THE SAN DIEGO GENEALOGICAL SOCIETY NEWSLETTER. Studio 30, Spanish Village, Balboa Park, San Diego, CA 92101	L	Q	
SAN DIEGO LEAVES AND SAPLINGS. San Diego Genealogical Society, Studio 30, Spanish Village, Balboa Park, San Diego, CA 92101	L	Q	
SAN FRANCISCO HISTORIC RECORD AND GENEALOGY BULLETIN. 1963-65. Louis J. Rasmussen, Colma, CA	L	IR	
SANGAMON COUNTY GENEALOGICAL SOCIETY QUARTERLY. P.O. Box 2298, Springfield, IL 62705	L	Q	
SANTA CLARA COUNTY HISTORICAL AND GENEALOGICAL SOCIETY. 2635 Homestead Road, Santa Clara, CA 95051	L	Q	
SANTA MARIA VALLEY GENEALOGICAL SOCIETY QUARTERLY. P.O. Box 1215, Santa Maria, CA 93454	L	Q	
SASKATCHEWAN GENEALOGICAL SOCIETY BULLETIN. Box 1894, Regina, Saskatchewan S4P 3E1	L	Q	

Select List of Periodicals

TITLE OF PERIODICAL, ADDRESS	SCOPE	FREQUENCY OF PUBLICATION	PRIORITY
THE SEARCHER. Southern California Genealogical Society, Inc., P.O. Box 7665, Bixby Knolls Station, Long Beach, CA 90807	I	Q	**
SEATTLE GENEALOGICAL SOCIETY SEARCH AND PROVE. Seattle Genealogical Society, Inc., P.O. Box 549, Seattle, WA 98111	N	Q	
THE SEEKER. Crawford County Genealogical Society, c/o Pittsburg Public Library, 211 West 4th Street, Pittsburg, KS 66762	L	Q	
SEQUOIA GENEALOGICAL SOCIETY, INC., NEWSLETTER. P.O. Box 3473, Visalia, CA 93277	L	M	
THE SETTLER. Bradford County Historical Society, 21 Main Street, Towanda, PA 18848	L	Q	
SETTLERS OF NORTHEAST ALABAMA. Mrs. Robert N. Mann, ed., P.O. Box 57, Cedar Bluff, AL 35959	L	Q	
SISKIYOU COUNTY GENEALOGICAL SOCIETY BULLETIN. P.O. Box 225, Yreka, CA 96097	L	Q	
SOMERSET COUNTY HISTORICAL QUARTERLY. Somerset Historical Publications, P.O. Box 146, Raritan, NJ 08869	L	Q	
THE SONOMA SEARCHER. Sonoma County Genealogical Society, 1019 Kenmore Lane, Santa Rosa, CA 95401	L	Q	

TITLE OF PERIODICAL, ADDRESS	SCOPE	FREQUENCY OF PUBLICATION	PRIORITY
THE SONS OF THE AMERICAN REVOLUTION MAGAZINE. National Society of The Sons of the American Revolution, 2412 Massachusetts Avenue, N.W., Washington, DC 20008	S/N	Q	
SONS OF THE REVOLUTION IN STATE OF VIRGINIA SEMI-ANNUAL MAGAZINE. 1922–32. Sons of the Revolution in State of Virginia, Richmond, VA	L	SA	
SOUTH BEND AREA GENEALOGICAL SOCIETY, 53139 Oakmont Park West, South Bend, IN 46637	L	Q	
THE SOUTH CAROLINA HISTORICAL AND GENEALOGICAL MAGAZINE. See THE SOUTH CAROLINA HISTORICAL MAGAZINE			
THE SOUTH CAROLINA HISTORICAL MAGAZINE (formerly THE SOUTH CAROLINA HISTORICAL AND GENEALOGICAL MAGAZINE). South Carolina Historical Society, Charleston, SC 29401	L	Q	
THE SOUTH CAROLINA MAGAZINE OF ANCESTRAL RESEARCH. Laurence K. Wells, ed., Box 694, Kingstree, SC 29556	L	Q	
SOUTH CENTRAL KENTUCKY HISTORICAL AND GENEALOGICAL SOCIETY, INC. QUARTERLY. P.O. Box 80, Glasgow, KY 42141	L	Q	
SOUTH FLORIDA PIONEERS, Richard M. Livingston, ed., P.O. Box 166, Ft. Ogden, FL 33842	L	Q	

TITLE OF PERIODICAL, ADDRESS	SCOPE	FREQUENCY OF PUBLICATION	PRIORITY
THE SOUTH JERSEY GENEALOGIST. William B. Brown III, ed., Willingboro, NJ	L	B	
SOUTH SUBURBAN GENEALOGICAL AND HISTORICAL SOCIETY. P.O. Box 96, South Holland, IL 60473	L	Q	
SOUTH TEXAS GENEALOGICAL AND HISTORICAL SOCIETY. QUARTERLY. P.O. Box 40, Gonzales, TX 78629	L	SA	
SOUTHERN ARIZONA GENEALOGICAL SOCIETY BULLETIN. See COPPER STATE BULLETIN			
SOUTHERN CALIFORNIA GENEALOGICAL SOCIETY, INC., BULLETIN. P.O. Box 7665, Bixby Station, Long Beach, CA 90807	L	Q	
THE SOUTHERN GENEALOGIST'S EXCHANGE QUARTERLY. Nancy L. Parker, ed., 4305 Coquina Drive South, Jacksonville, FL 32250	R	Q	**
THE SOUTHERNER. Southern States Chapter of the Utah Genealogical Association, P.O. Box 6028, Salt Lake City, UT 84106	R	Q	**
SOUTHSUBKIN. P.O. Box 96, South Holland, IL 60473	L	Q	
THE SOUTHWESTERN GENEALOGIST. Southwestern Genealogical Library, 5301 Hanawalt Drive, El Paso, TX 79903	R	B	
SOU'WESTER. Pacific County Historical Society, Box 384, Raymond, WA 98577	L	Q	

TITLE OF PERIODICAL, ADDRESS	SCOPE	FREQUENCY OF PUBLICATION	PRIORITY
SPRAGUE'S JOURNAL OF MAINE HISTORY. 1913-25. John Francis Sprague, ed., Dover-Foxcroft, ME	L	Q	
STALKIN' KIN. San Angelo Genealogical and Historical Society, Inc., P.O. Box 3453, San Angelo, TX 76901	L	Q	
STAMFORD GENEALOGICAL SOCIETY BULLETIN. 1958-71 (continued by CONNECTICUT ANCESTRY). P.O. Box 249, Stamford, CT 06901	L	4/yr	
THE STATEN ISLAND HISTORIAN. Staten Island Historical Society, Richmondtown, Staten Island, NY 10306	L	Q	
STIRPES. Texas State Genealogical Society, "Hacienda Tejas," 2515 Sweetbrier Drive, Dallas, TX 75228	N	Q	**
SUCCESS. Inez G. Von Harten, ed., 3364 Londonberry Place, Santa Clara, CA 95050	N/S	Q	
SUFFOLK COUNTY HISTORICAL SOCIETY REGISTER. 300 West Main Street, Riverhead, Long Island, NY 11901	L	Q	
THE SWEDISH PIONEER HISTORICAL QUARTERLY. Swedish Pioneer Historical Society, Inc., 5125 North Spaulding Avenue, Chicago, IL 60625	S/E	Q	
SYCAMORE LEAVES. Wabash Valley Genealogical Society, Inc., P.O. Box 85, Terre Haute, IN 47808	L	Q	

TITLE OF PERIODICAL, ADDRESS	SCOPE	FREQUENCY OF PUBLICATION	PRIORITY
THE TALLOW LIGHT. Washington County Historical Society, Inc., 401 Aurora Street, Marietta, OH 45750	L	Q	
TAP ROOTS. Genealogical Society of East Alabama, Inc., Box 45, Hurtsboro, AL 36860	L	Q	
TAYLOR COUNTY, IOWA, GENEA- LOGICAL GROUP. c/o Mrs. E.J. Janson, Box 8, Gravity, IA 50848	L	A	
THE TENNESSEE RESEARCHER. 1962- 65. Allstates Research Co., West Jordan, UT	L	Q	
TEXARKANA USA QUARTERLY. 901 State Line Avenue, Texarkana, AR 75501	L	Q	
THE TEXAS GULF HISTORICAL AND BIOGRAPHICAL RECORD. P.O. Box 1621, Beaumont, TX 77704	L	IR	
TEXAS HERITAGE. Texas Family Heritage, Inc., P.O. Box 17007, Ft. Worth, TX 76102	L	Q	
THEAKIKI. Kankakee Valley Genea- logical Society, 304 South Indiana, Kankakee, IL 60901	L	Q	
"THEY WERE HERE" GEORGIA GENEALOGICAL RECORDS. Frances Wynd, ed., 2009 Gail Avenue, Albany, GA 31707	L	Q	
THREADS OF LIFE. Lamesa Area Genealogical Society, P.O. Box 1090, Lamesa, TX 79331	L	Q	

TITLE OF PERIODICAL, ADDRESS	SCOPE	FREQUENCY OF PUBLICATION	PRIORITY
TIDEWATER VIRGINIA GENEA-LOGICAL SOCIETY. BULLETIN. Drawer K, Riverdale P.O., Hampton, VA 23366	L	Q	
TIMBERTOWN LOG. Saginaw Genealogical Society, c/o Saginaw Public Library, 505 Janes Avenue, Saginaw, MI 48607	L	Q	
TIPPAH COUNTY HISTORICAL AND GENEALOGICAL SOCIETY. NEWS-LETTER. 308 North Commerce Street, Ripley, MS 38663	L	M	
TOLEDOT, THE JOURNAL OF JEWISH GENEALOGY. P.O. Box 126, Flushing, NY 11367	E/S	Q	
THE TOPEKA GENEALOGICAL SO-CIETY QUARTERLY. P.O. Box 4048, Topeka, KS 66604	L	Q	
TORONTO TREE. Toronto Branch, Ontario Genealogical Society, Box 74, Station U, Toronto, Ontario M8Z 5M4	L	Q	
THE TRACKERS (formerly THE FORUM QUARTERLY and THE MT. HOOD TRACKERS). Mt. Hood Genealogical Forum of Clackamas County, Oregon, P.O. Box 703, Oregon City, OR 97045	L	Q	
TRAILS. North Alabama Genealogi-cal Society, Decatur, AL 35601	L	Q	
TRAILS WEST. Parker County Genea-logical Society, 1214 Charles Street, Weatherford, TX 76086	L	Q	

TITLE OF PERIODICAL, ADDRESS	SCOPE	FREQUENCY OF PUBLICATION	PRIORITY
TREASURE STATE LINES. Great Falls Genealogy Society, 1405 2d Avenue, N.W., Great Falls, MT 59404	L	Q	
TREE TALKS. Central New York Genealogical Society, Box 104, Colvin Station, Syracuse, NY 13205	L	Q	**
THE TREESEARCHER. Kansas Genealogical Society, Box 103, Dodge City, KS 67801	L	Q	
THE TREESHAKER. 1963-70. Permian Basin Genealogical Society, Inc., Odessa, TX	L	SA	
THE TRI-CITY GENEALOGICAL SOCIETY BULLETIN. Route 1, Box 191, Richland, WA 99352	L	Q	
TRI-STATE TRADER (Genealogy Section). Mayhill Publications, P.O. Box 90, Knightstown, IN 46148 (weekly newspaper)	R	W	**
TULSA ANNALS. Tulsa Genealogical Society, P.O. Box 585, Tulsa, OK 74101	R	3/yr	
TYLER'S QUARTERLY HISTORICAL AND GENEALOGICAL MAGAZINE. 1919-52. Richmond Press, Richmond, VA	I	Q	
UKIAH TREE TRACERS GENEALOGICAL SOCIETY. P.O. Box 72, Ukiah, CA 95482	L	Q	
THE UTAH GENEALOGICAL AND HISTORICAL MAGAZINE. 1910-40. Genealogical Society of Utah, Salt Lake City, UT	I	Q	

TITLE OF PERIODICAL, ADDRESS	SCOPE	FREQUENCY OF PUBLICATION	PRIORITY
UTAH GENEALOGICAL ASSOCIA-TION NEWSLETTER. P.O. Box 1144, Salt Lake City, UT 84110	I	M	*
VALLEY LEAVES. Tennessee Valley Genealogical Society, Inc., P.O. Box 1512, Huntsville, AL 35807	L	Q	
VALLEY QUARTERLY. San Bernard-ino Genealogical Society, P.O. Box 2505, San Bernardino, CA 92406	L	Q	
THE VINELAND HISTORICAL MAGA-ZINE. Vineland Historical and Antiquarian Society, Vineland, NJ	L	IR	
VIRGINIA GENEALOGICAL SO-CIETY QUARTERLY. Box 1397, Richmond, VA 23211	L	Q	
THE VIRGINIA GENEALOGIST. John Frederick Dorman, ed., Box 4883, Washington, DC 20008	L	Q	**
THE VIRGINIA MAGAZINE OF HISTORY AND BIOGRAPHY. Vir-ginia Historical Society, Box 7311, Richmond, VA 23221	L	Q	
WARREN COUNTY REFLECTIONS. Warren County Historical Society, Box 176, Williamsport, IN 47993	L	Q	
WATERLOO HISTORICAL SOCIETY. 131 William Street, Waterloo, Ontario N2L 1K2	L	A	
WEST-CENTRAL KENTUCKY FAMILY RESEARCH ASSOCIATION. THE BULLETIN. P.O. Box 1465, Owensboro, KY 42301	L	10/yr	

TITLE OF PERIODICAL, ADDRESS	SCOPE	FREQUENCY OF PUBLICATION	PRIORITY
WEST VIRGINIA ECHOER. 398 National Road, Wheeling, WV 26003	L	B	
THE WESTERN LINK. Western Texas Genealogical Association, 1916 23d Street, Snyder, TX 79549	L	Q	
WESTERN NEW YORK GENEA- LOGICAL SOCIETY JOURNAL. c/o Mrs. Harold J. Miller, 209 Nassau Avenue, Kenmore, NY 14217	L	Q	
WESTERN ONTARIO HISTORY NUG- GETS (formerly WESTERN ONTARIO HISTORICAL NOTES). University of Western Ontario Library, London, Ontario (discontinued)	L	SA	
WESTERN PENNSYLVANIA GENEA- LOGICAL QUARTERLY. Samuel C. Reed, Jr., 4338 Bigelow Boulevard, Pittsburgh, PA 15213	L	Q	
WHATCOM GENEALOGICAL SO- CIETY BULLETIN. P.O. Box 1493, Bellingham, WA 98225	L	Q	
WHERE THE TRAILS CROSS. South Suburban Genealogical and Historical Society, P.O. Box 96, South Holland, IL 60473	L	Q	
WHITE COUNTY HERITAGE. White County Historical Society, Box 327, Searcy, AR 72143	L	Q	
WHITE RIVER VALLEY HISTORICAL QUARTERLY. Box 565, Point Look- out, MO 65726	L	Q	
WILKES GENEALOGICAL SOCIETY, INC. BULLETIN. P.O. Box 1629, North Wilkesboro, NC 28659	L	Q	

TITLE OF PERIODICAL, ADDRESS	SCOPE	FREQUENCY OF PUBLICATION	PRIORITY
THE WILLIAM AND MARY QUAR-TERLY (also entitled WILLIAM AND MARY COLLEGE QUARTERLY). Institute of Early American History and Culture, Box 220, Williamsburg, VA 23185	N	Q	
WISCONSIN HELPER. Harriet A. and Walter L. Van Brocklin, 2941 South 56th Street, Milwaukee WI 53219	L	Q	
WISCONSIN STATE GENEALOGICAL SOCIETY NEWSLETTER. P.O. Box 90068, Milwaukee, WI 53202	L	Q	
WORLD RECORDS (formerly RECORD ROUNDUP). Genealogical Accredited Researchers, vols. 1-3, 1968-70. Rowene T. Obert, vols. 4-6, 1971-73.	I	Q	
YAKIMA VALLEY GENEALOGICAL SOCIETY BULLETIN. P.O. Box 2967, Yakima, WA 98902	L	Q	
YELLOWED PAGES. Southeast Texas Genealogical and Historical Society, 2870 Driftwood Lane, Beaumont, TX 77703	L	Q	
YESTERYEARS. Box 2, Poplar Ridge, NY 13139	L	Q	
THE YORK PIONEER. York Pioneer and Historical Society, P.O. Box 481, Station K, Toronto, Ontario M4P 2G9	L	SA	
YOUR ANCESTORS. 1947-59. Harry Ferris Johnston, Buffalo, NY	N	Q	
YOUR FAMILY TREE. Hoenstine Rental Library, P.O. Box 208, Hollidaysburg, PA 16648	L	Q	

Appendix 4

SAMPLE SURVEY CALENDAR

Shown here is an example of a survey calendar (log) which the genealogist could utilize in his recordkeeping system while performing a survey on a pedigree problem. This survey calendar will serve as a checklist and reminder that these indexes and sources should be searched when beginning most genealogical problems in American research.

If an item of interest is located in one of the periodical indexes, the researcher should make an extract of the entry--either a written extract or a photocopy-- and place an appropriate remark in the "Results" column of the survey log. Or, if no pertinent entry is located in the periodical indexes, write "Nil" in the results column. The genealogist should then locate the serial of interest for more data on the entry found in the index.

After systematically searching the available composite periodical indexes, the survey calendar should be maintained by the researcher along with other forms used in the notekeeping system. Similar logs could also be prepared by the researcher for other frequently used sources, such as THE AMERICAN GENEA-LOGICAL-BIOGRAPHICAL INDEX. Survey calendars serve as reminders to search sources in a systematic order.

Listed in the top half of this sample calendar are the titles of the major composite indexes to American genealogical periodicals. Space remains on the calendar for the researcher to list individual indexes to selected periodicals which might contain solutions to the pedigree problem, such as the indexes to the NATIONAL GENEALOGICAL SOCIETY QUARTERLY.

SURVEY CALENDAR

PATRON   DATE

NAME(S) OF INTEREST

LOCALITY OR JURISDICTION

LIBRARY CALL NUMBER	SOURCE DESCRIPTION	RESULTS
	GENEALOGICAL PERIODICAL ANNUAL INDEX (GPAI) current volumes Vols. 1–8, 1962–69	
	* St. Louis Genealogical Society. TOPICAL INDEX OF GENEALOGICAL QUARTERLIES, 1973-- .	
	* Waldenmaier, Inez. ANNUAL INDEX TO GENEALOGICAL PERIODICALS AND FAMILY HISTORIES, 1956-62	
	Jacobus, Donald Lines. INDEX TO GENEA-LOGICAL PERIODICALS, 3 vols.	
	Munsell, Joel. INDEX TO AMERICAN GENEALOGIES, 5th ed. 1900; also SUPPLE-MENT, 1900–1908	
	* QUERY NAME INDEX (QNI), 1973-75	
	* LINKAGE FOR ANCESTRAL RESEARCH (LFAR), 1967-- .	
	OTHER COMPOSITE AND SPECIALIZED GENEALOGICAL PERIODICAL INDEXES:	
(*Has limited value compared to other composite periodical indexes.)		

AUTHOR INDEX

In addition to names of authors and coauthors, this index includes all editors and compilers cited in the text. Authors of articles are also indexed. Omitted are names of editors or publishers of periodicals. Entries refer to page numbers in the text.

R

S

T

U

V

W

Z

TITLE INDEX

This index includes titles of books, published sources, theses, periodical indexes, and other sources cited in the text. In some cases the titles have been shortened. Periodicals, newspapers, and titles of articles are not indexed, except those major titles which are the subject of a chapter or section. The periodical titles in appendix 3 are not listed in this index. Entries refer to page numbers in the text.

A

B

Title Index

C

Calendar of Virginia State Papers and Other Manuscripts 110
Canadian Index to Periodicals and Documentary Films 113
Canadian Periodical Index 113
Catalogue of American Genealogies in the Library of the Long Island Historical Society 107
Catalogue of the Genealogical and Historical Library of the Colonial Dames of the State of New York 102-3
Christian-Evangelist Index, 1863-1958, The 103
Civil War Index 103
Climbing Our Family Tree Systematically 9
Consolidated Bibliography of County Histories in Fifty States in 1961 40
County Courthouse Records 31
County Courthouses and Records of Maryland, The 28, 30
Cumulated Magazine Subject Index, 1907-1949 103-4, 113
Cumulative Author Index for Pool's Index to Periodical Literature, 1802-1906 114
Cumulative Index to a Selected List of Periodicals 114

D

Dictionary Catalog of the Local History and Genealogy Division 123
Directory of Genealogical Periodicals, A 121
Directory of Genealogical Societies in the U.S.A. and Canada 121-22
Directory, Genealogical Societies and Periodicals in the United States 88, 118-19
Directory, Historical Societies and Agencies in the United States and Canada 118

E

Education Index 114
Essay and General Literature Index 114

F

Family History for Fun and Profit 8
Family Surname Publications 121
Finding Your Forefathers in America 6
Founders of Early American Families 103
Fundamentals of Genealogical Research 7

G

Genealogical & Local History Books in Print 109, 123
Genealogical Books in Print 109, 123-24
Genealogical Dictionary of Maine and New Hampshire 107
Genealogical Index, The 107-8
Genealogical Material and Local Histories in the St. Louis Public Library 109
Genealogical Newsletter and Research Aids 51-57
Genealogical Periodical Annual Index 59-69, 76, 78, 90-92, 96-99, 119, 124
Genealogical Periodicals: A Neglected Treasure 31, 68
Genealogical Reader: Northeastern United States and Canada 9
Genealogical Reader, The 11, 20, 29
Genealogical Research 6
Genealogical Research Essentials 9
Genealogical Research Standards 7, 20
Genealogical Research: A Jurisdictional Approach 7
Genealogies in the Library of Congress 36, 40, 120-21

SUBJECT INDEX

All major subject areas have been indexed. In some cases titles of published sources and authors are included here if they are the subject of a chapter or section. Most references are to American genealogical and historical sources. See and see also cross references have also been used. Entries refer to page numbers in the text.

Subject Index

Correspondence 3
County histories. See Local histories, indexes to
Cross-references in indexes 21-22, 25
Cumulative index to genealogical periodicals 95, 97-98

D

Delaware, sources in 108
Detroit Society for Genealogical Research Magazine, The 17-18
Direct locality approach 26, 89
Directories of genealogical societies 118-25
Directory of genealogical and historical periodicals 55
Disciples of Christ Historical Society 103

E

Errors. See Printed sources, errors in
Ethnic periodicals 16
Evidence, evaluating 2
Examples for genealogical periodicals 89-94

F

Family and home sources 2-4
Family and local history 1
Family Bibles. See Bible records, indexes to
Family histories
bibliography of 120-21
indexes to 33-40, 54
title pages to 40
Family newsletters 16
Family organizations 16
Family periodicals
bibliographies of 120-21, 123-24
indexes to 59-69, 77-88
Family traditions 3
Future periodical indexing 98-99

G

Genealogical Newsletter and Research Aids 51-57
Genealogical Periodical Annual Index 59-69
Genealogical periodical indexes, using 25-27, 89-94, 95-99
Genealogical periodicals
bibliographies of 117-25
contents of 13-14
frequency of publication 128-81
indexes to 1, 4, 22-32, 95-99, 101-15
limitations of 14-15
list of titles 127-81
recommended titles 18
scope of 15-16, 127-81
suggested holdings for libraries 128-81
types of 15-16
value of 11-20
Genealogical queries. See Queries
Genealogical research, aspects of 1-9
Genealogical research method 2
Genealogical research, systematic method of 1-9
Genealogical societies in North America 121-22
Genealogical Society Library, Salt Lake City 4, 9, 96, 99, 111-12, 117, 122
Genealogical survey. See Survey phase
Genealogies, documented 14-15
Genealogies. See Family histories
Genealogists. See Accredited Genealogists; Certified Genealogists
Genealogist's Weekly Query Index 78-80
Genealogy, definition of 5
German-American sources 118
Goals. See Objectives, selecting

H

Haverford College Library 105-6
Hereditary organizations 120
Historical periodicals 18-19
bibliographies of 117-25
indexes to 33-40, 43-49, 101-15

Subject Index

T

U

V

W